the Smart Approach to

baby
rooms

CREATIVE
HOMEOWNER®

the Smart Approach to
baby
rooms

Joanne Still
Principal Photography by Mark Samu

CREATIVE HOMEOWNER®, Upper Saddle River, New Jersey

VP/Editorial Director: Timothy O. Bakke
Production Manager: Kimberly H. Vivas

Senior Editor, Decorating: Kathie Robitz
Photo Editor: Jennifer Ramcke
Editorial Assistant: Jennifer Doolittle

Senior Designer: Glee Barre
Illustrator: Janet Kroenke

Photography (unless otherwise noted): Mark Samu
Front Cover Photography: courtesy of Blue Mountain Wallcoverings
Cover Design: Glee Barre
Back Cover Photography: (clockwise) courtesy of York Wallcoverings; courtesy of Thibaut Wallcoverings; courtesy of Lambs & Ivy

Printed in the United States of America

Current Printing (last digit)
10 9 8 7 6 5 4 3 2 1

The Smart Approach to Baby Rooms
Library of Congress Catalog Card Number:
2004103420

ISBN: 1-58011-113-0

CREATIVE HOMEOWNER®
A Division of Federal Marketing Corp.
24 Park Way
Upper Saddle River, NJ 07458
www.creativehomeowner.com

ACKNOWLEDGMENTS

Many thanks to those who gave generous support and assistance in the development and writing of this book. In particular, I would like to recognize Paula Markowitz, President and CEO of the juvenile bedding manufacturing company PatchKraft. Paula provided many leads and much information on safety issues regarding infant and juvenile products across the board, including—but not limited to—furniture and bedding. Paula's personal and professional advocacy for infant and child safety sets an industry benchmark.

I would also like to say special thanks to educator and child development specialist Marie Lysandrou for her research help.

And not least, thanks to the four Still kids—Joseph Jr., Caitlyn, Jared, and Savannah—for being an inspiration.

CONTENTS

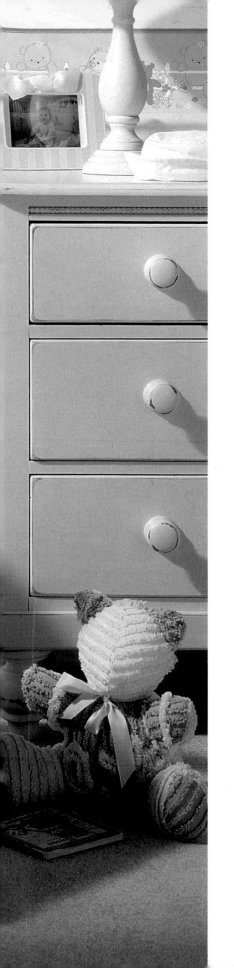

INTRODUCTION

A walk through any baby boutique or specialty store can seem like a trip through a wonderland of nursery- and infant-related products. *The Smart Approach to Baby Rooms* represents one way to deal with the "idea overload" that comes with it. This book will show you how to systematize and simplify the design process while keeping it fun during this special time. In it, you'll find everything you need to know about creating your baby's first room and making it a beautiful, peaceful haven.

Chapter 1, "Sweet Dreams," pages 12–31, discusses a range of topics, from the issue of sleeping arrangements to important facts about bedding, including mattresses and bumpers. And because prevention of sudden infant death syndrome (SIDS) is a vital concern for all parents, guidelines are included for reducing its risk.

Experts say that visual stimulation is important for brain development, so Chapter 2, "Color Their World," pages 32–45, offers a brief primer on the science of color, along with smart advice about how to use it creatively. You'll find advice for choosing a color scheme, how to coordinate prints and solids, as well as painting tips for the novice do-it-yourselfer to ensure the best results.

Feel lost when you try to imagine the overall project? Read Chapter 3, "Plans and Schemes," pages 46–63. It covers basic design concepts, starting with scale and proportion, and walks you through some of the hands-on work that is essential to planning and designing a space, including the steps to creating a floor plan and how to arrange furniture pleasingly, even in the tightest quarters.

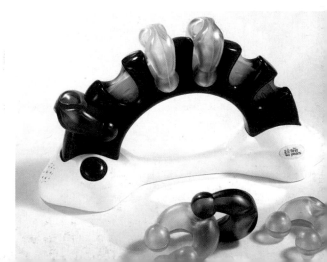

Children grow so fast, and the quietly sleeping infant in the nursery today will be an active toddler before you know it. That's why Chapter 4, "Ideas for Toddler Rooms," pages 64–83, takes a peek into the future and helps you plan ahead. Here's how to make smart decisions that can save you money, time, and energy as you adapt your little one's space to his ever-growing requirements.

How much furniture do you need for the nursery? Not much, but Chapter 5, "Furniture and Storage," pages 84–103, will explain what is necessary and include tips for investing in quality furniture that will last beyond your baby's first years. You'll find creative ideas for storage, too.

In Chapter 6, "Wall and Window Treatments," pages 104–127, you'll get great ideas for adding style with everything from paint and wallpaper to curtains, shades, and blinds. You'll also find useful guidelines for estimating paint and wallpaper needs.

Don't forget what's underfoot. Chapter 7, "Flooring for the Nursery," pages 128–145, takes a look at all of the practical options for the nursery, with advice on care.

Whether you're registering for shower gifts or shopping for yourself, Chapter 8, "Accessories and Necessities," pages 146–161, outlines some of the other products and devices that you'll want for the nursery.

Most accidents that result in injury can be prevented. Chapter 9, "Safe in Any Room," pages 162–173, covers important safety information that you need to know. Planning a nursery for a child with special challenges is addressed in Chapter 10, "Meeting Special Needs," pages 174–185.

The "Appendix," pages 186–191, offers furniture templates and graph paper to help you plot your design.

Finally, the Resource Guide, page 192, is an important listing of manufacturers and industry-related associations. Addresses, e-mail contact information, and telephone numbers make this a handy reference guide.

The Smart Approach to Baby Rooms is packed with photographs to illustrate every one of the ideas under discussion. Within them, you are sure to find inspiration for your own project. Also, be sure to check the "Gallery of Smart Ideas," a photo album that follows every chapter. Each "Gallery" is a visual shopping spree combined with a designer's flair for enhancing both form and function.

Left: A wallpaper pattern of little feet is an adorable way to transform any space into a room for the baby.

Opposite: Today's cribs and linens are manufactured with your infant's safety and comfort in mind.

SWEET DREAMS

WHERE WILL THE BABY SLEEP?
▪ BEDDING, BEAUTIFUL AND SAFE

For the first few months, your baby will spend most of every day sleeping. The typical newborn sleeps about 16 to 18 hours out of every 24, waking every two to four hours or more to be fed. Between 1 month and 2 years of age, a baby's total sleep time gradually decreases, from an average of 15 hours down to about 13 hours.

Even the youngest infants have individual needs. Basically, they sleep when they want, and there's not much you can do to make them fall asleep or to wake them for that matter. That said, most babies will sleep best in a darkened, quiet room. Although you might find it convenient to keep a night light on in the nursery so that you can see what you're doing when you go into the room, the baby is fine sleeping in the dark and, in fact, may sleep better without a light. Little ones don't become afraid of the dark until 2 or 3 years of age, when they begin to be able to think in abstract concepts—including the idea of "scary things" in dark corners and under the bed.

If the nursery must be close to the area of your home where a lot of living happens, it's a good idea to buffer sudden, loud noises. Keep a radio on in the baby's room tuned to a spot on the dial that gets only static and turn the volume down low enough to create background noise. Tapes and CDs are also available that provide background nature sounds, such as constant breaking of waves against a shoreline or a stream running over rocks. However, it's not a good idea to tiptoe around the house while your baby is sleeping; she will adjust soon to the normal sounds and noises of everyday family living.

Above: Use bookcases to display favorite items. Other details that will make the room more inviting include glass cabinets, above right, decorative shelves, right and below, and colorful toys. Set up a crib, opposite, even if the baby sleeps with you at first.

WHERE WILL THE BABY SLEEP?

There are several options for your newborn's sleeping arrangements: a bassinet, cradle, crib, or even the "family bed." Some new parents choose a co-sleeping arrangement, with the baby sleeping in their bed for the first few weeks. This is a controversial practice: some experts claim that co-sleeping (or sleep sharing) increases the risk of sudden infant death syndrome (SIDS), while others say the evidence is weak for such a link, and still others argue that co-sleeping actually reduces the risk of SIDS. If you are considering co-sleeping, it's a good idea to discuss this with your pediatrician. If you decide to have the baby share the family bed—on a conventional mattress, never on a waterbed—check with the American SIDS Institute (listed in the "Resource Guide," on page 192) for safety precautions.

Even parents who choose co-sleeping for the first few weeks or months of the baby's life usually choose to move the baby out of the family bed or to a nursery at some point.

Whenever you decide to do this, it's important to have a good sturdy crib and mattress ready and waiting. So allow plenty of time for delivery of the crib before the baby arrives. Pretty details and decorations are fine, but your newborn won't notice any of those things for the first few months. For the time being, his or her instincts are to sleep and eat, and then sleep some more.

You should be thinking about your baby's sleeping arrangements before he arrives. Here are some things you can do to help with your decision.

SMART steps

ONE Decide on the type of bed. Bassinets and cradles can be used only for a few months of infancy. Cribs are usually used until a child is between 2 and 3 years old. According to the Sleep Products Safety Council (SPSC), once a child is 35 inches tall, she should make the transition from crib to bed.

If you choose to purchase a new crib, do you plan to have more children who can use it later? If not, what will you do with the crib when your child graduates to a bed? Unless you have specific plans that make the investment in a crib worthwhile, it may be more cost-effective to consider purchasing a convertible model (one that can be used as a bed later) that will last your child for years.

TWO Buy the best-quality mattress you can afford. The difference between the least-expensive foam product and the top-of-the-line innerspring mattress can be as little as $60. If you are on a tight budget, this is not where you should pinch pennies. Remember, important developmental things are occurring during you baby's sleep.

THREE Do a safety check. If the crib or bassinet is a hand-me-down, make sure that it conforms to

Opposite: Many cribs convert to junior beds, so you won't need to purchase another bed as your child outgrows the crib. When making the conversion, check the condition of the mattress.

Right, top: Your instincts will tell you when your child is ready for a bed, but as a guide, consider making the switch when your child reaches 35 in. tall.

Right: Although you will be attracted to a crib's styling, for safety's sake, look for a seal from the Juvenile Products Manufacturers Association.

Left: Many babies spend their first few months of life in a bassinet before moving to a crib. If you plan on taking the bassinet outdoors, be sure it has a hood, such as the one shown here, to keep the sun out of the baby's eyes.

SMARTtip Mobile Safety

To prevent accidental strangulation, mobiles and other crib toys strung from rail to rail should be removed once the baby is 5 months old or is able to push herself up onto her hands and knees, whichever comes first. Another option is to hang all mobiles from the ceiling, out of the baby's reach.

the current safety standards, discussed later in this chapter; a new crib must be manufactured according to those standards. Whether the crib is new or used, review the recommendations for safe bedding to prevent smothering, overheating, and the risk of SIDS. Check the fit of the mattress: it should be snug against the crib—no more than two fingers' width between the mattress and the side of the crib.

BASSINETS

For the first few months of an infant's life, many parents choose to have him sleep in a bassinet, a relatively light, woven basket in a stand. If the idea of a bassinet is appealing, choose one that can be lifted easily out of the stand for easy transportation from room to room or outdoors on a pleasant day. (Most have a hood for shielding the baby's eyes from light.) The bassinet can be left in your bedroom or can be moved there during the night, making nighttime feedings less disruptive. Because a bassinet is only suitable for the first few months, consider borrowing one. However, when borrowing a bassinet, buy a new mattress, which should be firm and fit snugly.

Cradles. A cradle, which looks like a hybrid of a small crib and a rocking chair, is another small-bed alternative to a crib for newborns. They are usually made of wood and measure roughly 18 by 36 inches. The side-to-side motion of a cradle is soothing to babies, which may be one reason that many families have heirloom cradles passed down from generation to generation. A baby can usually sleep in a cradle for about the first four months. Again, a new mattress is a must. It should be firm and at least 2 inches thick.

CRIBS

Even if a newborn's first months are spent in a bassinet or cradle, she eventually will spend most of her sleep time in a crib. Cribs come in a large variety of styles, dimensions, and finishes, and your choice should be based on how the piece will help to create the overall look of the room. For this reason, you'll need to decide on your basic room decor before choosing a crib. In addition, you may want to think long-term and take a look at cribs that convert to junior beds (also called youth beds) and, later, as your child grows, even twin- or full-size beds.

A nice safety feature—although not a requirement—in some new cribs with solid end panels is a slit for bumper ties. When shopping for a crib, look for this slit because it makes installation of the bumpers much easier.

A crib should be sturdy and properly assembled, and it should meet current safety standards. This is a simple matter with a new crib: it should carry the safety certification seal from the Juvenile Products Manufacturers Association (JPMA), which ensures that the piece meets national standards. However, an heirloom piece that has been in the family for years or that wonderful antique you bought at an auction requires some careful scrutiny and may not be safe for use in your baby's nursery.

Above and Below: Cradles come in a variety of designs, but they all allow you to slowly rock your baby to sleep. Cradles are usually portable, allowing you to let the baby nap in a room other than his bedroom.

To determine whether an older or vintage crib is service-able, make sure that the headboard and footboard have no decorative cutouts and that the crib has no corner-post extensions or finials. Slats should be spaced no more than 2⅜ inches apart—about the diameter of a can of soda. Check for loose parts or missing pieces. If the crib is paint-ed, consider whether lead-based paint might have been used; if in doubt, a complete stripping, sanding, and refin-ishing job is in order.

Mattresses. Whether the crib is vintage or not, the mattress should be new. The Consumer Product Safety Commission (CPSC) advises that mattresses should fit snugly so that the baby cannot become trapped between the mattress and the frame. If you can fit two fingers between the mattress and the side of the crib, the mattress is too small.

To properly support the baby's growing body—and to pre-vent smothering—mattresses should be firm. Two types of crib mattresses are available: foam and innerspring.

Light and relatively inexpensive, *foam mattresses* are made of polyester or polyether. They come in a variety of thicknesses and densities. The best-quality, longest-wearing foam mat-tress you can buy has a high-density that is roughly 1 pound per cubic foot.

Innerspring mattresses (also known as coil mattresses) tend to maintain their shape over the long term better than most foam mattresses. This is important because your child will be sleeping in a crib for at least two years. As with inner-spring mattresses for twin-, full-, queen-, and king-sized beds, those made for cribs owe their firmness to several fac-tors, such as the number of turns per coil and the temper for the wire used to make the coils. The most important factor, however, is the number of coils. For a crib mattress, the ideal minimum is 150.

When shopping for a mattress, also look at the ticking and the venting. Double-laminated (or even better, triple-lami-nated) ticking with nylon reinforcement will resist mois-ture. This type of ticking is also durable over time. Make sure the mattress has enough vent holes to allow air to cir-

culate and permit odors to escape; this is important for long-term freshness of the mattress.

BEDDING, BEAUTIFUL AND SAFE

Soft, billowy blankets, comforters, sheets, or pillows should not be placed in the crib with a baby. These items pose a risk for smothering. In addition, overheating has been asso-ciated with an increased risk of SIDS. (See "Reducing the Risk of SIDS," page 24.) Furthermore, rebreathing exhaled carbon dioxide has been linked with SIDS; this is one rea-

Above left: **A properly sized mattress fits snugly against the crib's frame. If you can fit two fingers between the mattress and the rail, the mattress is too small.**

Above: **Slats on the crib should be no more than $2\,^{3}/_{8}$ in. apart. There should be no sharp edges on the crib.**

son that babies should always be placed on their backs rather than their stomachs to sleep. When putting the baby in the crib, keep pillows and heavy blankets away from him because having plenty of room for fresh air to circulate around him is important.

To keep the baby warm, dress her in a snuggly sleeper—an excellent example is a so-called "wearable blanket,"which is like a sack made of microfleece. (See "Resource Guide," on page 192.) If additional covering is needed, use small, thin blankets of flannel or polar fleece, and ensure that these are securely fastened.

SMARTtip   Bedding Safety

Any blankets and bumpers should be thin, flat, and fastened securely to minimize the risk of covering your baby's head or face.

The best fabrics for baby bedding are tight-weave cotton or cotton blends (such cotton and polyester). Chenille is a poor choice of fabrics for a baby's bedding. Natural development involves a baby's increasing ability to explore his environment with fingers and mouth. Chenille is a soft-pile rather than a woven fabric, and the soft tufts that feel so luxurious can be pulled loose and ingested by a curious infant. As a result, the CPSC has determined that chenille poses a risk for gagging, and some experts think that future research may show that this fabric increases the risk for choking. In addition, even frequently laundered chenille is a haven for dust mites.

Bumpers. Thick, rounded, puffy bumpers are pretty and soft to look at, but they have been shown to pose a safety hazard to babies and should not be used in cribs. Never use bumpers as loose pillows. When you install them, make sure they are tight and firmly secured.

The issue of bumper ties is another area of concern for parents. Some efforts were made several years ago to mandate a standard size for the strings that attach bumpers securely to the crib. JPMA and the juvenile products division of the American Society for Testing and Materials (ASTM) have determined that the safest length for bumper ties is between 7 and 9 inches.

The minimum length, 7 inches, may be too short to fit around the rails or posts in some cribs, but 9 inches will work for most—keeping the bumpers securely fastened to the crib and preventing them from flopping around in the crib. This is a voluntary standard adhered to by some manufacturers, but it is up to consumers to purchase and use products that conform to these requirements. The safest bumpers have ties for the four corners of the crib, and on both the top and bottom of the bumpers.

Left: The best fabrics for crib bedding are a tightly woven cotton or a cotton and polyester blend. The Consumer Product Safety Commission has determined that chenille can be dangerous because the baby can ingest and choke on the tufts.

Reducing the Risk of SIDS

Sudden infant death syndrome (SIDS) is defined as the unexplained death of a baby under one year old. The rate of SIDS has fallen by 50 percent since 1983, the year that research and educational efforts were started to try and reduce the number of these tragic events. Nevertheless, approximately 25,000 SIDS deaths still occur each year. The search is still on for the cause—or more likely, the causes—of SIDS, but a number of risk factors have been identified. According to the SIDS Alliance, following some guidelines in the nursery can help reduce the risk of SIDS: One of the first principles that emerged from SIDS research was that babies should always be placed on their backs to sleep.

■ The baby should be put to sleep on a firm, flat mattress. (See the section on "Mattresses" on page 20 for more information.) Avoid soft sleeping surfaces—for example, don't ever let your baby sleep on a waterbed.

■ Overheating increases the risk for SIDS. Keep the temperature in the baby's room between 60 and 70 degrees Fahrenheit. Signs of overheating include sweating, damp hair, and restlessness.

■ Keep pillows, fluffy blankets, and stuffed toys out of the crib.

■ Don't allow anyone to smoke cigarettes around your baby—not just in the nursery, but anywhere in your home. The risk of SIDS increases with the amount of exposure to cigarette smoke.

This page and opposite: Bedding for the nursery should be washable and soft. Run your hands over it before buying to make sure that there are no snags and no attachments that can choke the baby or make him uncomfortable. You'll find attractive coodinated sets like these in affordable price ranges. For your baby's comfort, shop for linens that are all cotton or a cotton-polyester blend.

a gallery of

1 Toys and mobiles hung from crib railings can add color to the bedroom and help keep the baby occupied. When the baby is about 5 months old or is able to push herself up on her hands and knees, remove rail-hung items for safety.

2 Purchasing a crib and mattress can be expensive, but some models are convertible, meaning they can be used as the baby's first real bed rather than go into storage when he outgrows the crib. When making the change, consider redesigning the room with new bedding, furniture, and accessories as shown here.

3 Although they will help your child develop, don't think stuffed animals are for your baby's enjoyment only. They are an inexpensive way to accessorize and add color to a space. They also help make a room seem more homey and inviting. Just remember to remove them from the crib when the baby is in it.

4 There are a lot of ways to pull the design of a room together, but shown here is an inexpensive one that is effective. The homeowners started with neutral-color walls and rug and simple furniture that is paint-

smart ideas

ed white. The room gets its look from the repeated use of the print on the fabric; it is used as a window treatment, canopy for the crib, and cover on the easy chair.

5 Designing a baby's room gives you the chance to have some real fun and take some real chances. After all, the room is for a baby, so it should be unlike any other space in the house. In what other room would you even think of putting up wallpaper—or painting a wall stencil—with a teddy bear and crescent moon theme? Be warned, though, your child will outgrow the design, even if you don't.

a gallery of smart

ideas

1 Even though your baby may not be old enough to appreciate your efforts, make the nursery as you would like it.

2 A soothing color scheme is one way to create an environment for sleeping.

3 Vintage wicker can be sweet for a newborn's room.

4 Comfortable, washable linens can add style as well as practicality to the nursery.

a gallery of

1 Make sure that the crib is sturdy and adjustable to three or four different mattress heights to accommodate your baby as she grows.

2 An antique crib may have sentimental value, but it should conform to updated safety recommendations. Any crib should also be easy to operate.

3 Provide age-recommended, stimulating toys for your baby in and around the crib.

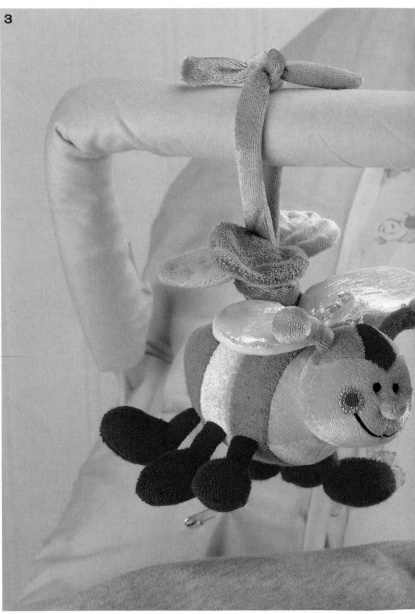

smart ideas

4 A Beatrix Potter theme is carried over from the wallcovering to the crib linens. Many juvenile wallpaper lines can be coordinated with sheets and quilts.

5 Once your baby is old enough to stand himself up in a crib, it's time to move him into a bed. If the crib converts into a toddler bed, you're set. Otherwise, shop for an adult-size bed, or put the mattress on the floor until you're ready for the bed purchase.

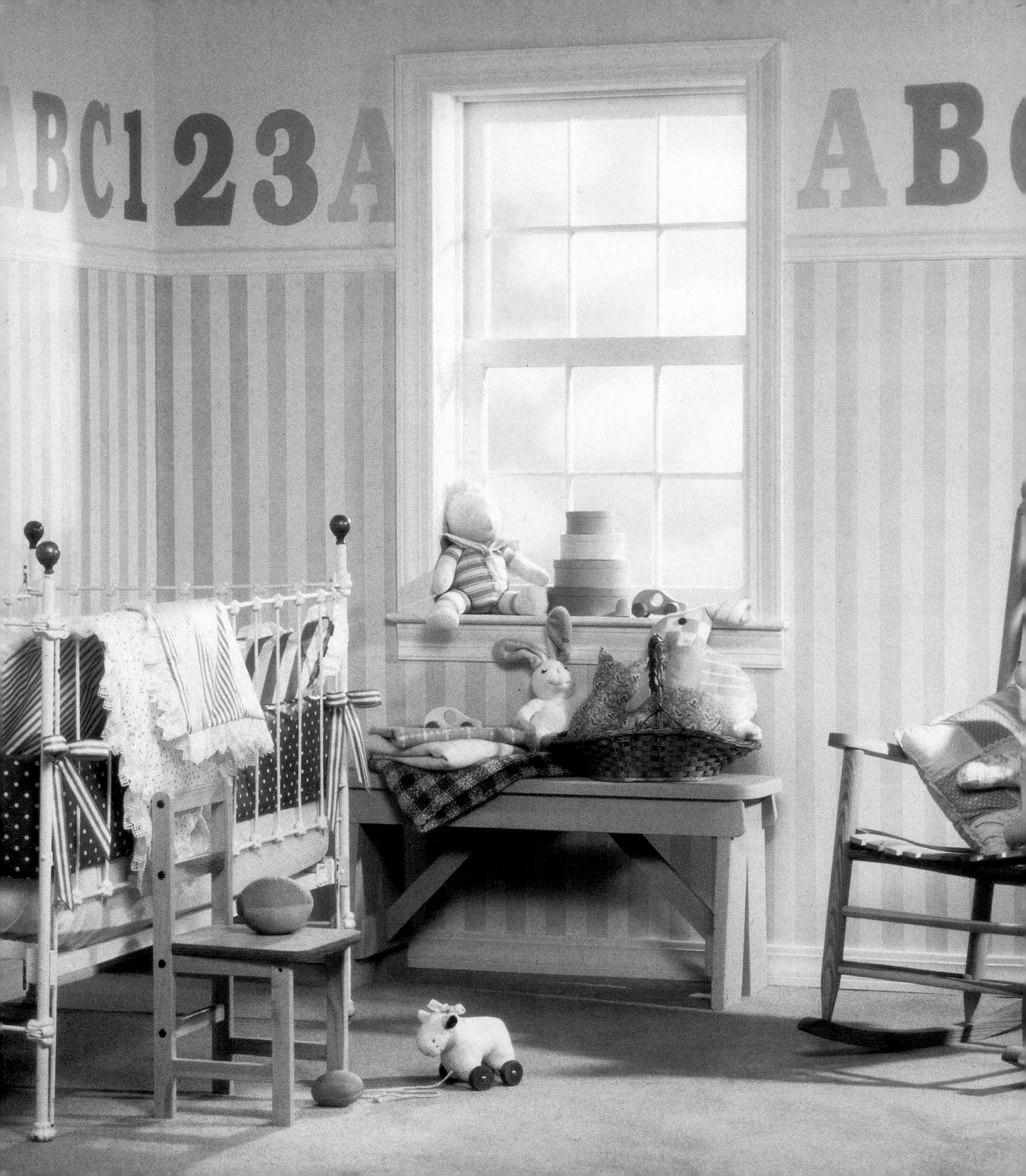
ABC123A
ABC

CHAPTER 2

COLOR THEIR WORLD

A PALETTE OF POSSIBILITIES
■ DEVELOPING A COLOR SCHEME
■ LIGHT AND COLOR ■ COLOR AND CHILD DEVELOPMENT

Put simply, color is light of different wavelengths, which humans perceive through sensors in the retina of the eye. Light reflected through a prism creates the "color spectrum," bands of color that range from red—the longest wavelength—to orange, yellow, green, blue, and violet. This spectrum is also evident in rainbows, when we're fortunate enough to witness the right combination of sunlight and the natural prism formed by moisture in the air following a rain shower.

Modern color theory transformed those sequential bands of color into a useful tool known as the color wheel. This is a circle that shows the relationship of one color to another and can be used for pairing colors. In the color wheel, colors are divided into primary (red, yellow, and blue), secondary (green, orange, violet), and tertiary colors (such as red-blue and blue-red). Secondary colors are created by mixing two primary colors (red and blue to make purple, for example). Tertiary colors are formed by mixing a primary and a secondary color; for instance, turquoise is created by mixing blue and green.

In considering a color scheme, another factor to understand is *intensity*. This is the level of the color's (or hue's) purity or saturation. Primary, secondary, and tertiary colors are full-intensity. To lessen the intensity of any color, you can add white, black, or gray to it. The addition of white to any color lightens it and forms what is called a *tint*. When you add black to a color, you've created a *shade* of that hue. The addition of gray forms a *tone*. In color-theory parlance, these methods of changing color intensity affect what is known as the color's *value*—tinting creates a light value, whereas shading gives a color a darker value.

As you think about possible colors for the nursery, the physical dimensions and the design of the room should come into play, because color can affect the perception of the space, how it feels, as well as how large or small it seems. You don't need a science lesson to use color to good advantage, just a few pointers that may be helpful when you're developing your color schemes. For example, if the baby's room is large, make it cozy with warm colors, which visually advance. The perceived size of a room also can be reduced with the use of sharp contrasts or darker colors. If the room is small, cool colors or neutrals visually recede, which will make the room feel larger.

Monochromatic, or single-color, schemes and neutrals of similar *value* (lightness or darkness) also seem to make the walls recede. By lessening a color's intensity, the tendency to advance or recede is affected as well.

A PALETTE OF POSSIBILITIES

Developing a palette for the nursery may be one of the easiest things you have to do. But if you're not confident about picking colors, it can be a challenge. Rather than giving up and painting everything white, how about trying to develop your artistic sense and getting creative? Here's a little background information to get you started.

DEVELOPING A COLOR SCHEME

A color scheme is a combination of colors, one that can be derived by a process of trial and error, which is not a bad thing. Or, you can play it safe and take a studied approach using the color wheel (below) as a guide. Don't be put off by fancy words, such as monochromatic or tetrad. You'll see, using the color wheel is very easy.

First, choose a basic color; use the color wheel to develop a scheme that works with that main hue. The types of schemes include monochromatic, analogous, complementary, triadic, split-complementary, and tetrad.

Monochromatic Schemes. A palette of one color only is a monochromatic scheme, such as all-blue or all-green.

Opposite: Equal parts of cool blue and warm yellow create a pleasing balance in this room. Introducing a lesser amount of the color pink, with accessories, adds more complexity to the overall scheme.

CHOOSING A SCHEME WITH STAYING POWER

By the time your child is a toddler, she will have a very definite opinion about the colors she prefers, evidenced by her choices when reaching for toys and, later, coloring pictures and choosing clothing to wear for the day's activities. Meanwhile, the choice is yours.

But what if you select a moderately intense color scheme and you find, later, that your older baby needs the calming effects of more gentle hues? Or if you chose a soft pastel scheme for the nursery and two years later your toddler expresses a clear preference for the exciting visual stimulation of pure primary colors, what should you do? No problem. Color schemes can be changed easily with toys, linens, or accessories. Furthermore, a fresh coat of paint is relatively inexpensive. So don't be afraid to make the nursery any color you like until then. Remember, there are very few rules, as a child's room can be just about any combination of colors and patterns imaginable. Decorate with flexibility, as your child's interests will develop at the same rate as she does. A child's room is the perfect place to use daring and artistic ideas, so whether you choose vivid color combinations or softer pastels, don't be afraid to let your own imagination run free.

SMARTtip   Natural Light

The quality of natural light is a big consideration when choosing colors for your child's room. Be prepared for the shade you choose to take on a little different hue as the day progresses. Artificial light and different window treatments will help you change the effects or adjust the level of light in the room as needed.

Right: A scheme composed of primary colors—red, blue, and yellow—is always popular in a child's room. Here they are used in their boldest, truest forms, with red and blue doing a balancing act, while yellow takes the role of accent color.

a gallery of smart ideas

1 A lively wallpaper print looks cheerful. Solid-color accents anchor the scheme.

2 Painted effects and murals offer an opportunity to add color and pattern.

3 Blue walls always create a peaceful look that's conducive to rest.

4 For interest, paint a second color on an angled wall or ceiling.

5 A border can act as a transition between the top and bottom wall treatments.

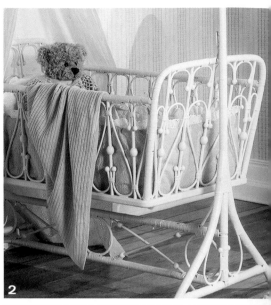

1 Painted white furniture lets you get more creative with other surfaces in the room. The border just under the ceiling line draws the eye upward.

2 Although they have gender-specific connotations, pastel shades of pink and blue continue to be favored, especially in the traditional nursery.

3 Creative uses of color may include painted murals for the wall, the ceiling, or even on the front of a chest of drawers.

4 To enliven a color scheme, add contrasting or complementary colors to the doors or on the window trim.

5 Play up a monochromatic, or single-color, theme by using various tints and shades of the same hue.

a gallery of smart ideas

Rhythm. Rhythm is repetition of pattern or shape. Repeated forms help to pull someone's visual attention around the room, keeping the look of the room interesting rather than static.

Now that you know how to look at space and the objects that can fill it, you can begin the real process of design on your own. The following Smart Steps can lead you through the process.

Below: A well-designed room will contain accessories that support the overall color scheme. Notice how this fanciful chess set works with the rest of the room.

SMART steps

ONE Measure the room. Using a steel measuring tape, measure the dimensions of the room and write them down. Also record the sizes of openings—the door or archway to the room, windows, closet doors—as well as any unmovable features, such as built-in shelving or drawers. Note the positions of electrical switches and outlets, phone jacks, radiators, heat registers, air ducts, and light fixtures.

If you already have some furniture pieces that you think you'd like to include in the nursery, measure those too.

Then, draw a freehand sketch using the measurements you've made. Include all of the elements above.

TWO Draw a floor plan to scale. Now, using your best "art class" skills, create a floor plan on graph paper. A plan drawn to scale is an invaluable reference when you're furniture shopping or considering how you'd like to arrange the layout of the room. To keep your sketch neat and readable, use shorthand for measurements—for example, 4'5" for 4 feet, 5 inches—and use standard symbols to indicate permanent features such as built-in bookcases and closets. The standard symbols are shown in the Appendix, on page 186.

Quad-ruled graph paper is best. With this type of ruling (4 squares to the inch, on paper) the squares are small enough to make the finished product manageable yet large enough to allow you to work easily with furniture templates, as discussed in Step 3. For drawing your floor plan, you'll need a ruler or straightedge plus a sharp pencil and eraser. Using your sketch

C H A P T E R   3

PLANS AND SCHEMES

DESIGN BASICS
■ ADDING IT ALL UP ■ WORKING WITH PROFESSIONALS

First impressions mean a lot, and that's true from the time a baby arrives in her new world. You'll want your baby's environment to be as special as she is, as cozy, warm, and inviting as she deserves.

Where can you find ideas to inspire you to choose just the right look for the nursery? In addition to the room designs shown in this book, check out home decorating magazines, and take some field trips to stores in your area that carry juvenile furniture. Visit the large chain stores, but don't overlook any smaller establishments that might offer creative displays of their merchandise.

If you own or have access to a personal computer, ideas are just a click away online at countless Web sites: explore the Web pages of trade associations, manufacturers of juvenile furniture, wallpaper, and other decorating elements, and major on-line shopping outlets.

Many new parents have all or some of the skills and sufficient time to create the baby space of their dreams. Others need some assistance with the design or execution of their ideas. Whatever the level of your design know-how, you need to keep some basics in mind before you start thinking

DESIGN BASICS

You don't need to be a professional designer to furnish and decorate your baby's new space. For the best result, however, it doesn't hurt to understand the basic concepts and the language of design. Having a few basics in mind will help you feel more confident so that you can enhance both your skills and your own sense of style.

A RELIABLE FRAMEWORK

Many people simply don't know where to begin when they're shopping for furniture or choosing fabrics and patterns for the home. Selecting items for baby's room is not an exception, especially when the room is small. But you can't go wrong if you apply the decorating principles of scale and proportion, line, balance, harmony, and rhythm.

Scale and Proportion. These two principles work together. *Scale* is the size of something (for example, a nursery) in relation to the size of everything else (a house). A nursery

Left: You will be buying your baby's first toys, offering you the chance to use them in the overall design of the room.

Below: The ceiling lines combined with the shape of the window emphasize this room's tall ceilings.

Opposite: Wallpaper with a complementary border shows the design concept of harmony.

specifically about colors, furniture, window treatments, and the like. This chapter, will cover a few basic concepts of design that will help you in everything from arranging furniture to choosing window treatments. You'll also learn how to take a critical look at the space you've designated for the nursery, and trying different arrangements, on paper, for making the space work for you and your baby. The idea, by the end of this process, is to be organized enough to decide whether you'll do all or some of the work yourself and what, if anything, you'll leave to a professional. Finally, you'll learn how to put together a realistic budget before you finalize your plans.

of a particular size could be perceived as large or small depending on the overall size of the house. *Proportion* is the relationship of things to one another based on size. For example, a chest may be too big for a particular room.

Line. Lines define and shape space, and convey visual messages. The vertical line where two walls meet, for example, defines that corner of a room. Lines can be used to create a perception. Vertical lines appear strong, whereas horizontal lines appear restful. Diagonal lines suggest motion and transition, and curved lines express softness.

Balance. The even placement of things of varying sizes shapes around a room is known as balance. Many peo assume that balance requires symmetry—that there is that says if you do something to one side of an object, must do the same thing to the other side of that objec However, balance can be asymmetrical, as well, with p ing and often more interesting results.

Harmony. When everything in a space coordinates wit one scheme or motif, the result is referred to as harmo This is the principle that pulls a room together.

PLANS AND SCHEMES

DESIGN BASICS
■ ADDING IT ALL UP ■ WORKING WITH PROFESSIONALS

First impressions mean a lot, and that's true from the time a baby arrives in her new world. You'll want your baby's environment to be as special as she is, as cozy, warm, and inviting as she deserves.

Where can you find ideas to inspire you to choose just the right look for the nursery? In addition to the room designs shown in this book, check out home decorating magazines, and take some field trips to stores in your area that carry juvenile furniture. Visit the large chain stores, but don't overlook any smaller establishments that might offer creative displays of their merchandise.

If you own or have access to a personal computer, ideas are just a click away online at countless Web sites: explore the Web pages of trade associations, manufacturers of juvenile furniture, wallpaper, and other decorating elements, and major on-line shopping outlets.

Many new parents have all or some of the skills and sufficient time to create the baby space of their dreams. Others need some assistance with the design or execution of their ideas. Whatever the level of your design know-how, you need to keep some basics in mind before you start thinking

DESIGN BASICS

You don't need to be a professional designer to furnish and decorate your baby's new space. For the best result, however, it doesn't hurt to understand the basic concepts and the language of design. Having a few basics in mind will help you feel more confident so that you can enhance both your skills and your own sense of style.

A RELIABLE FRAMEWORK

Many people simply don't know where to begin when they're shopping for furniture or choosing fabrics and patterns for the home. Selecting items for baby's room is not an exception, especially when the room is small. But you can't go wrong if you apply the decorating principles of scale and proportion, line, balance, harmony, and rhythm.

Scale and Proportion. These two principles work together. *Scale* is the size of something (for example, a nursery) in relation to the size of everything else (a house). A nursery

Left: You will be buying your baby's first toys, offering you the chance to use them in the overall design of the room.

Below: The ceiling lines combined with the shape of the window emphasize this room's tall ceilings.

Opposite: Wallpaper with a complementary border shows the design concept of harmony.

specifically about colors, furniture, window treatments, and the like. This chapter, will cover a few basic concepts of design that will help you in everything from arranging furniture to choosing window treatments. You'll also learn how to take a critical look at the space you've designated for the nursery, and trying different arrangements, on paper, for making the space work for you and your baby. The idea, by the end of this process, is to be organized enough to decide whether you'll do all or some of the work yourself and what, if anything, you'll leave to a professional. Finally, you'll learn how to put together a realistic budget before you finalize your plans.

of a particular size could be perceived as large or small depending on the overall size of the house. *Proportion* is the relationship of things to one another based on size. For example, a chest may be too big for a particular room.

Line. Lines define and shape space, and convey visual messages. The vertical line where two walls meet, for example, defines that corner of a room. Lines can be used to create a perception. Vertical lines appear strong, whereas horizontal lines appear restful. Diagonal lines suggest motion and transition, and curved lines express softness.

Balance. The even placement of things of varying sizes and shapes around a room is known as balance. Many people assume that balance requires symmetry—that there is a rule that says if you do something to one side of an object, you must do the same thing to the other side of that object. However, balance can be asymmetrical, as well, with pleasing and often more interesting results.

Harmony. When everything in a space coordinates with one scheme or motif, the result is referred to as harmony. This is the principle that pulls a room together.

Rhythm. Rhythm is repetition of pattern or shape. Repeated forms help to pull someone's visual attention around the room, keeping the look of the room interesting rather than static.

Now that you know how to look at space and the objects that can fill it, you can begin the real process of design on your own. The following Smart Steps can lead you through the process.

Below: **A well-designed room will contain accessories that support the overall color scheme. Notice how this fanciful chess set works with the rest of the room.**

SMART steps

ONE Measure the room. Using a steel measuring tape, measure the dimensions of the room and write them down. Also record the sizes of openings—the door or archway to the room, windows, closet doors—as well as any unmovable features, such as built-in shelving or drawers. Note the positions of electrical switches and outlets, phone jacks, radiators, heat registers, air ducts, and light fixtures.

If you already have some furniture pieces that you think you'd like to include in the nursery, measure those too.

Then, draw a freehand sketch using the measurements you've made. Include all of the elements above.

TWO Draw a floor plan to scale. Now, using your best "art class" skills, create a floor plan on graph paper. A plan drawn to scale is an invaluable reference when you're furniture shopping or considering how you'd like to arrange the layout of the room. To keep your sketch neat and readable, use shorthand for measurements—for example, 4'5" for 4 feet, 5 inches—and use standard symbols to indicate permanent features such as built-in bookcases and closets. The standard symbols are shown in the Appendix, on page 186.

Quad-ruled graph paper is best. With this type of ruling (4 squares to the inch, on paper) the squares are small enough to make the finished product manageable yet large enough to allow you to work easily with furniture templates, as discussed in Step 3. For drawing your floor plan, you'll need a ruler or straightedge plus a sharp pencil and eraser. Using your sketch

as a guide, record the measurements you made onto the graph paper, letting each square of the paper represent one foot. (If a wall measures 10 feet, for example, the line you draw to show that wall will take 10 squares.)

THREE List the main furniture needs, and make templates for the floor plan. You know the basic furniture pieces that will be in your baby's room: a crib; a changing table; a place to store clothing, toys, and other necessities; and perhaps a small table to provide a surface for the baby monitor, a lamp, and other items. Measure the items you already own and, adjusting for the actual size of your pieces, draw and cut out templates, using those in the Appendix as a guide.

If you are planning to buy any of these or other pieces, cut out templates based on the standard sizes provided in the Appendix, and know that you will need to get the exact dimensions of each piece of furniture before you buy it. Guessing about size can lead to costly mistakes. The salesperson can provide you with manufacturers' spec sheets.

Top: Plan furniture placement before buying the pieces. You will need templates for the crib and changing table to place on your floor plan.

Right: This built-in changing table contains handy diaper storage. Later it can be used as a dressing area for an older child.

FOUR Try out furniture arrangements. Spend some time trying different configurations of the templates on the floor plan. In addition to merely fitting the pieces, consider the basic design concepts that were discussed on pages 48-50.

Also, create a focal point by starting with the largest piece first. In a nursery, this usually is the crib. The focal point is the one element that grabs your attention when you first walk into a room. Then play with the rest of the layout and furniture, taking allowances for clearance into consideration

Opposite: **On your floor plan, place the crib first and work out from there.**

Right: **Plan storage for dozens of small toys and playthings.**

SMARTtip

How Much Space Do You Need?

How do you know if a room will be too crowded? Will there be enough space for the built-in drawers to be usable if you put the changing table near the door? Here are some rules of thumb on clearances of items typically found in a baby's room. If possible,

■ maintain 40 inches of space into the room to open drawers without blocking a traffic aisle.

■ reserve 3 feet of space in front of a closet to allow the door to open easily.

■ keep 22 inches of clear space around the crib.

■ leave 6 inches between furniture and baseboard heating and air-conditioning units.

And don't forget: allow room for access to wall outlets and light switches.

Who Should Do the Work?

Is it realistic for you to do all the work yourself? Or should you hire a professional contractor? Perhaps the answer is some combination of the two. To make an honest evaluation, consider these eight questions.

1. **How big is the project?** If the room requires only cosmetic help to make it baby-ready, even a novice with sufficient interest can pick up the necessary skills. An individual who has some experience with makeovers can certainly do a fine job. However, when some special work—such as electrical wiring or painting a mural, below and below right—needs to be done, hire a professional.

2. **Do you have enough time to commit to the project?** You can probably paint the walls in a weekend, but think about how much time it will take to shop for, order, and assemble new furniture, or to strip down and repaint vintage pieces. If you're also working full-time outside the home or if you have small children to take care of, these time-consuming tasks can get overwhelming pretty quickly.

3. **Do you have the temperament to get the whole project done yourself?** If you are naturally patient and persistent and enjoy the process of things, the do-it-yourself route may be perfect for you. However, if you become impatient when the bolt and nut don't easily fit where the directions say they should or the chair rail, above, isn't plumb, you won't fully enjoy what should be a delightful experience. If you tend to get frustrated by snags, ask for (or hire) help. Don't start something you won't be able to finish.

4. **Do you enjoy—and are you able to do—physical work?** If you have some experience with removing and hanging wallpaper, installing flooring

ADDING IT ALL UP

Before you set your plan in motion—or even set your plan firmly in your mind—develop a budget for the project. First, if a baby shower is planned for you, make a wish list of everything you'd like for the room. Take a look at store or on-line registry lists. The items on these lists are conveniently organized into categories, and they include prices. You may not want to sign up for a registry, but shower guests usually ask the hostess for some suggestions for gifts, and having the list from a registry can be extremely helpful. If you've already had a shower or you have things from older siblings lovingly stashed away for this baby, catalog those items. Then list the things that you're likely to need brand new, along with their prices.

WORKING WITH PROFESSIONALS

Aside from furniture and accessories, you'll need to consider professional fees. Even die-hard do-it-yourselfers agree that seeking professional help is sometimes the most cost-effective way to get a job accomplished. After considering—and honestly answering—the questions here, determine the areas in which you are likely to require professional help, either from a designer or a contractor.

Interior designers can turn an expert eye on a space and your belongings and often can rearrange or reuse many of the things you already own. Even if you have a practiced design sense of

---

material, or refinishing furniture, you know what tasks you can do and which you enjoy (or don't). If these are new to you and your design plan calls for such skills, it may be a good idea to enlist the help of a friend who has been through the paces. With the materials, tools, and instructional help available today, don't automatically rule out doing it without professional help. You can probably pick up the know-how quickly with a little hands-on guidance from an experienced do-it-yourselfer or by attending a workshop at a home center.

5. **Have you ever done any of this kind of work before?** Even if you are a complete novice, it's not impossible for you to accomplish wonders, but you have to ask yourself how much you want to struggle. See questions 1 and 4.

6. **Do you have the tools you'll need to do specific jobs?** Hanging wallpaper, installing window shades, even painting stripes, below, all require tools. If you don't already have them, can you borrow them? If you'd need to purchase them, consider whether it would be less expensive to hire a professional.

7. **Can you get help if you need it?** Sometimes a task requires more than two hands. Will someone be available to lend a hand or two when you need it? Also, do you have a knowledgeable source on whom you can call if you have questions or run into problems you can't handle yourself?

8. **Does your plan and budget have enough "wiggle room"** in it so that it can be adjusted in case you discover you can't do it yourself? If you hit a snag you can't handle, would you consider changing the plan? Or if you make a mistake you can't fix without assistance, you need to be prepared to call in someone to help you, and that may affect your budget.

your own, a professional can provide tips about arranging wall art, eliminating clutter, using color effectively, or coordinating prints and fabrics. Many of these experts will work on an hourly basis, particularly for a small space such as a nursery, and consultation fees can be reasonable—sometimes in the neighborhood of $100 an hour. Don't overlook the possibility of getting free design advice where you shop; sometimes this is provided as a free service for customers.

To determine how much to budget if you think you will be needing the services of a tradesperson such as a carpenter, painter, electrician, or wallpaper hanger, get two or three estimates. Most contractors will gladly provide one, and

their review of what your job entails will undoubtedly be educational for you. Whatever the final figure on the estimate, pad it! A 20 percent comfort zone isn't unreasonable. First, you never know what problem may come up that neither the contractor nor you can foresee. Second, the budget padding will allow for what might be called "better-way cost creep." That's when, in the middle of the job, the contractor says, "I can do it the way we discussed for the price we agreed on, or I can do it another, better way that will cost a little more."

Direction: **Three colorful lambs share a sunny spot near an open window. Select toys that are easy to keep clean.**

Visual Tricks for Modifying the Shape of a Room

Aside from doing major structural work, how do you deal with an oddly shaped room? Designers have developed some clever ways to disguise or draw attention away from jarring imperfections.

Long. If a room is long, divide the space by creating two or more separate groupings of furniture. For example, in the nursery, use the crib as the focal point for the sleeping area, right, then put a dresser, rocking chair, table, and lamp in separate section of the room.

Narrow. A narrow space can be made to seem wider by placing furniture on the diagonal. Place the crib

catercornered, and introduce as many squares as possible into the room. For example, group art in a square arrangement on the wall, use a cube-shaped chest, and hang a large, square-shaped mirror on a major wall.

Too Low. A room with a low ceiling can feel cramped and closed-in. In general, use as many vertical lines as possible to add height. A more expansive impression results with the use of tall, narrow bookcases or an armoire, for example. Height can also be added with the use of window treatments that hang from above the window frame or extend from just below the ceiling to the floor. Vertical stripes is a good pattern for such a room.

Too Tall. If the ceiling is too high, the scale of the space can be lowered by incorporating more horizontal lines in the room. For example, walls will appear shorter if molding is installed halfway or three-quarters of the way up. Also, hang pictures lower on walls.

Too Angular. Some rooms—such as those built under attic eaves—may appear chopped up because they have too many angles. To unify the spaces, choose one color or print for all surfaces, including the ceiling, or play up interesting angles with different treatments, left.

a gallery of smart ideas

1 Conservative furniture is for grownups; young children would rather have designs with which they can identify. Here a simple chest is painted with the image of a popular storybook character.

2 You may be surprised at what you might have in the garage or basement that can help in decorating the baby's room. A simple stepladder adds interest as a display stand for large toys. Paint your ladder a bright color.

3 Stenciling a colorful design on a wall provides a quick and rela-

tively inexpensive way to add color to a room. There are hundreds of stencils available at paint and craft stores. When you or your child tire of the design, simply change it by painting over the original and adding another.

4 When selecting furniture, plan on adding a few kid-size pieces. Your baby won't use them for some time, but they do add to the design of the child's room.

5 The same pattern used throughout this room helps to tie the overall design theme together.

a gallery of smart ideas

1 Need help coodinating the details? Some boutiques and baby specialty stores offer free or nominal-charge design advice.

2 Mix it up. Play with pattern and print to add interest to the room.

3 Paint or wallpaper the insides of shelves or cubbies for a custom look.

4 Apply a wallpaper border vertically along the side of a wall or around door or window trim.

a gallery of smart ideas

1 A small display shelf takes up little space but adds a special touch.

2 Put cute little outfits on display by hanging them on wall racks or pegs.

3 Make use of nooks and crannies, such as the space inside the wall between the studs.

4 Limit toys to a few things if space is tight. Rotate them if they are too cute to hide away.

5 Keep the room open to air and light, but don't neglect privacy.

CHAPTER 4

IDEAS FOR TODDLER ROOMS

GETTING STARTED ■ A ROOM PLAN ■ DECORATING FOR TODDLERS

A toddler, even a very young one, forms an attachment to his room and understands it clearly to be his own. He knows his clothes belong in the room, his toys live there, and every night it is where he comes to sleep. It's also likely the only room in the house where he is allowed to touch most of what he sees. So it's important to plan a room that not only pleases your child's senses but also serves his needs. This is a period of transition, from totally dependent baby to ever-more independent tot. It's the time for moving from crib to bed, for acquiring possessions, and for developing play skills. So in addition to the decorative elements you choose for the room, there are several other important factors that should be part of your game plan: buying a bed, determining storage needs, planning play space, and making the room safe.

By the age of 2, your child will demonstrate numerous likes and dislikes. You may be able to discern some of her preferences for specific colors and theme subjects by the toys she gets most excited about or particular articles of clothing she likes more than others. Although it's too early to assume that these favorites will last, you can use them as clues to help you design a room that reflects her personality and stimulates her imagination.

GETTING STARTED

The transition from nursery to a big boy's room can be a little disruptive for a toddler, even with his growing sense of independence. To counter any fears brought on by the change, gradually get your child used to the idea. Here's what you can do to prepare your youngster for the changes.

SMART steps

ONE Communicate. It's never too soon to start talking to your child. Explain that this is her room. Parents of toddler-age children have heard the word "mine" often enough to know that the promise of "ownership" is enticing to youngsters.

Right: Let your toddler's growing sense of self guide some of your decisions about the decorative aspects of the room. Take a cue from a favorite color or toy.

Below, left and right: By the age of around 2, a little one is ready to move from a crib into a big boy's bed. Keep some nursery items so that the new room is still familiar.

TWO Involve your child. Let your tot "help" you by bringing some of his things into the room, for example. Show him where his toys and clothes will go and ask him to put them away.

THREE Appeal to her pride. Emphasize that because she's not a baby anymore, she's going to sleep in a grownup bed now, and she'll have "big girl" furniture.

A ROOM PLAN

Room to play is probably the most important thing you can provide. Kids of this active age need rocking horses and indoor gym sets. If space permits, divide the room into sep-arate zones for sleeping, storytelling, making crafts, and playing. You may be able to contain some of the mess if, for instance, finger paints are permitted only at the crafts table (where snacks may be taken, too) and toys must remain in the play zone. You can visually partition the space by using different flooring types, such as carpeting near the bed, wood or a wood-laminate in the play zone, and resilient or vinyl flooring in the craft area.

Tight on space? Arrange all the furniture against the walls to free up floor space for playing in the center of the room. Look around and decide what you don't have to keep in the room. If floor space is at a premium, don't include a chair and side table in the plan for the time being. (You can sit next to your child in bed when you read to him.)

Above: Now it's time to begin showing your youngster that there is a place for everything. Choose furniture pieces that will encourage her to put things away after using them.

Right: Your toddler's favorite soft toy or stuffed animal can be comforting once she is finally out of the crib. Display them on the bed or keep them nearby.

SMARTtip — Essential Furnishings

Essential Furnishings Checklist. Start with these basics to get started. You don't have to buy everything on the list, but it will serve as a guideline for planning your budget.

- ■ Bed

- ■ Chest of Drawers

- ■ Toy Box

- ■ Nightstand

- ■ Lighting

- ■ Small Table and Chairs

- ■ Flooring

FURNISHINGS

If your crib converts to a toddler bed, you're pretty set, as the nursery dresser will likely suffice for the time being, as well. However, it's probably a more practical idea to buy an adult-size bed at this stage. With the addition of a child's table-and-chair set and toy storage, these items may be able to carry you and your little one through until she is about 5 or 6 years old.

The Bed. A twin-size adult bed is ideal, although you may have to buy a double bed somewhere down the line as your child gets older and wants to have friends for sleepovers. For a young toddler who is adjusting to a grownup bed, there are twin beds that come with guard rails that can be removed later. Why not a toddler bed? First, it may not have guard rails, although it is lower to the floor. Plus, a toddler bed is seldom constructed with box springs, which means it cannot provide the proper support your child

Right: Plan both storage and display areas with an eye to the future. As your child grows, so will her number of possessions.

If you are considering more furniture at this time, clean-lined designs that work with a variety of decorating styles are best. Beds with built-in storage are particularly practical. Furniture that is designed specifically for kids and has met the standards set forth by the Juvenile Products Manufacturers Association and the Consumer Products Safety Commission can be considered risk-free. But if you're looking at furniture designed for adults, take into consideration ornate woodwork that can cause injury by catching little arms and legs and any design elements that may present choking hazards.

What's more important is storage for all of the toys that start to accumulate at this age. When your tot gets tired of something, put it away in the attic, garage, or basement for a while and bring something else out.

Above, left: A headboard with built-in open and closed storage, a shelf for toys, and perhaps a bulletin board for art or photos create a compact, cozy environment for a toddler.

Below: If space allows, designate separate areas for sleep and play. If the room will be shared, built-in desks and cabinets will serve well into the adolescent or teen years.

needs. Shop for a twin mattress with at least 200 coils or a double-size that has at least 300 coils.

If you don't want to commit to a specific furniture style now, simply buy the twin-size frame, mattress, and box spring. A headboard and a footboard are optional items and can be added later if you want to coordinate the bed with other furniture in the room. Otherwise, something improvised, such as a stenciled design on the wall behind the bed, can be changed easily and is a good idea.

Well-constructed novelty beds can serve well, and may be passed from one child to the next. Although some youngsters may want a bed that's not childlike in a couple of years, novelty beds remain popular with most children until age 8 or 10.

Storage. One dresser is probably sufficient for a child this young. You can be the judge. Pass on the dresser mirror for the time being, or just put it in storage. Things tend to fly across young children's rooms, and a large mirror that can shatter is a potential disaster. Install one later when you feel your child is ready.

Above: Having a place to display pretty things or collections will teach a little one the importance of neatness and make it easier for her to put things away when they're not in use.

Below: A window seat with a hinged lid is an excellent way to create attractive storage and seating in a room. Washable fabrics for the cushion and pillows are practical.

Crates, cubbies, and plastic bins provide excellent toy storage. Kids get out of bed at night, and they can trip over objects left on the floor. Bins on wheels are handy for picking up at the end of the day. A traditional toy box is useful, but make sure it operates with safety hinges. If you want to use an old trunk or one that wasn't intended for toys, that's fine, as long as you retrofit it with safety hinges.

Shelves are always a good idea. If your child is a climber, a low shelf is an invitation to explore, and it may be dangerous. On the other hand, if you keep shelves low enough on the wall for your child to reach, you're helping him learn to pick up after himself. Adjustable shelves that rest on supports attached to wall-mounted steel brackets offer the most flexibility. Otherwise, plastic crates that can be used as cubbyholes may be affixed to the walls for storage. Anything heavy that can fall over, such as tall bookcases or other tall storage compartments, should be bolted securely to the walls as well.

For bulkier items, install a closet organizer. Easy-to-assemble wire-coated systems come in numerous configurations and include bins, baskets, drawers, and shelves. Lower hanging rods make it possible for kids to hang their clothing, as do children's clothes trees and pegged racks.

There is another option: custom-built storage, which will serve your child's needs for years to come. It's a good investment, particularly in a small room that defies organization. If you hire a professional carpenter, explain that you expect the pieces to accommodate your child's storage needs now (stuffed animals, storybooks, toys) and in the future (heavy textbooks, stereo equipment, perhaps a TV). Don't forget to get references and check them out. Then obtain several estimates for the work.

Small Table and Chairs. A tot-sized table-and-chair set provides a place for fantasy and creativity. Little ones like to get their fingers into things, and so this is where they can safely play with paints, crayons, clay, and other messy things. It can be a spot for light snacks and teddy bear tea parties, too. Sturdy plastic sets can take a real beating, and they can be scrubbed down without causing harm. You can buy a set made of wood, too, or look for an unfinished table and chairs that you can customize with paints. Use a semigloss paint, which you can wipe clean with a damp sponge.

Lighting. Lighting needs change as children grow. At this stage, good general lighting spread evenly around the room is necessary, as well as a soft night light that can be left on for the many times you may have to check on or tend to your little one. You'll need a reading light for storybook time, too. It can be near the bed or next to a chair, wherever you'll sit while reading. Task lighting for toddler-age children isn't necessary. Shorter attention spans and a lack of coordination make long-term concentration on one task rare at this time.

For good general lighting, install recessed or ceiling-mounted fixtures and a dimmer switch. A table lamp can be risky because it can be knocked down when small children become rambunctious. And running kids can trip on cords. Instead, you could use a wall-mounted fixture or sconce with a light source you can direct. Whatever the case, never put a lamp where a youngster can reach up and get injured by a hot bulb.

Flooring. Just as in a nursery, flooring for a toddler's room should be chosen with practicality in mind. Little ones spend a lot of time playing on the floor, and they spill stuff. You'll need a surface that can stand up to toys that are dragged from one end of the place to the other, one that can be swept and mopped up easily. That makes resilient flooring or a laminate product the most suitable. Wood, especially if it has been sealed with polyurethane, is easy to keep clean, although it may scratch, depending on the fin-

Above: Wall-to-wall carpeting is soft under tender little feet that will be on the go from morning until night. Check out stain-resistant brands.

ish. If you want it to stay looking good, invest in a finish that can be damp-mopped. For warmth underfoot near the bed, install an area rug with a skid-proof backing. Something you can pop into the washing machine makes sense, unless the area rug is large. In that case, regular vacuuming will take care if it.

Carpeting is another option, but one that may be better suited to an older child's room because it's not as easy to keep clean as other types of flooring. It may also pose a problem for children with allergies and asthma because it can harbor dust and other allergens, making regular daily vacuuming a must.

DECORATING FOR TODDLERS

Themes carried over from the nursery are still suitable for children in this age category. Depending on your nursery choices, you may not need to change the wall and floor treatments at all. Babyish themes will become inappropriate by the end of the toddler stage, but some may last well into the first couple of years or until school age.

If you're starting from scratch, a good place to begin is with color. At this stage, asking your child to choose a favorite is futile. She may give you an answer, but it's likely to change every time you ask. Studies, a bit more reliable than those conducted with babies, indicate that bright colors attract toddler-age children. Red and yellow, in particular, are stand-out favorites. In general, bright colors stimulate psychologically, while cool colors have a relaxing effect. You may want to experiment with the effect of various colors on

Below, left: Be careful about theme decorating. This log-cabin look has staying power that should last for years. The "logs" are actually wallpaper.

Right, top and bottom: Toy displays and accessories carry the the theme. Even the storage items suit the decor.

Above: A stenciled picket fence and flower garden is a cheerful theme for a little girl's room.

Right: A stenciled arbor creates a focal point behind the bed. White wicker furniture pulls the look together.

SMARTtip   Cute Beds

A well-constructed novelty bed, such as a "racing car," can be as decorative as it is practical.

your child. Try out a lively scheme if you think your child could use more stimulation in her development. Conversely, see what happens to your overly energetic tot when she's in a room of quiet, soft colors.

Pastel colors appear to be less appealing to toddlers than bright ones, but that doesn't mean you have to replace them if they already exist in the room. If you can easily make a change with a wallpaper border or new curtains, for example, that's great. But you're not going to do any harm by sticking with what you have. If you decide to make changes, go with geometric prints, stripes, plaids, or any other classic motif that isn't too youthful. That way the wallcoverings, curtains, and bed linens will last well

into the school years or until your child is tired of them. Because young children are more attracted by color than form, color is an excellent way to get your child excited about a new room. If you dislike bright or primary colors, choose a neutral overall scheme and accent it with bright red, blue, or yellow, or a combination. So many toys and accessories designed for children of this age are decorated in these colors, and that will make accessorizing the room easy. Another approach is to experiment with various tints and shades of one primary color to find attractive variations on a monochromatic (one-color) scheme. For example, try using different shades of blue for the walls, trim, window treatment, and bed linens. If you get tired of this later, just change the color of one of these elements.

TWO OR MORE TO A ROOM

At this age, it's not unusual for two children to share a room. If the co-occupants are nearly the same age, the arrangement is fairly easy. Each child should have a separate bed. An activity table can be shared as well as the play space. It's a good idea to provide separate toy storage for each youngster, but this can be as simple as assigning one toy box or shelf to each child. A bedside table at this age is not necessary, but it always comes in handy—even if it's just for a night light. For a symmetrical look, one shared table between twin beds is fine. Chairs or futons that convert to twin beds are another space-saving option. Look into beds that come with under-bed storage drawers.

A situation where a school-age child must share a room with a much younger brother or sister is more difficult, but sometimes unavoidable. For one thing, both children need their own separate area in the room. Plus, you have to provide storage for the older child that the toddler cannot access for his own safety. Share with your older child the job of seeing that dangerous items are kept out of reach. But remember that the safety of a younger sibling is too much responsibility for any child.

Avoid a decorating theme that is too youthful. Keep the motif neutral by avoiding wallpaper and fabrics with childish themes. Pick something that would be appropriate for any age, such as a floral print in a room shared by girls or plaid for a boys' room. Perhaps paint the walls a solid color instead. You can use accessories, such as a night light, soft wall art, and a few stuffed animals for the younger child's half of the room; then let your older child hang posters or prints on her side of the space.

Furniture that divides up the room is a good idea if there is enough space to allow for modular pieces. Otherwise, a folding screen will allow privacy for your older child. If necessary, it can be folded up during the day to allow light from windows on one side to spill into the entire room.

Above: Bunk beds are a practical idea when two kids must share a room. However, a bunk bed, especially one without a guard rail, may be too grown up for a toddler.

You can also divide the room in half visually by choosing two different themes. For example, if it's a boys' room, decorate with a baseball theme on one side and a hockey theme on the other side. Two themes for two girls could be dance and gymnastics. Or you could decorate with two totally different motifs as selected by each child. Use complementary color schemes to unify the two areas while providing visual separation. Anything you can do to make sure each child feels comfortable is helpful.

FINISHING TOUCHES

Refrain from adding too many accessories to a young child's room, especially if that includes delicate or small objects. The point is to make the space a free zone, where everything is touchable and safe. For example, because lower parts of walls traditionally take a beating from toddlers armed with crayons, chalk, and markers, why fight it? Instead, mask off a section, and paint it with chalkboard paint. This is a latex product that you can paint over later when you're ready to change the room again. Using chalk, little kids can draw and practice writing their ABCs to their hearts' delight. Plus, their scrawls and scribbles will be erasable, so they can create new ones over and over. Chalkboard paint can also be used to create a tabletop drawing surface or to decorate doors.

Another way to pack the room with personality is with decorative paint effects. Sponged-on or ragged finishes let you add something extra to ordinary painted walls, and the dabbed-on texture camouflages smudge marks and greasy little fingerprints. The walls can be painted over when your child is older and it is time to freshen and update the look of the room. Looking for an easy project? Try

Safety in the Toddler's Room

Toddlers seem to have a sixth sense that draws them like magnets to a potential source of harm. It's really just their natural curiosity and growing independence. Here's a list of things that you can do to keep them free from harm:

- Install caps and covers on all electrical outlets.

- Use window guards that restrict the size of and access through window openings.

- Tie or wrap up long cords on blinds and shades so that they have no loops and are out of reach.

- Use molded plastic electrical cord covers.

- Install devices in place of your switch-plate covers that lower the switch to a child's level.

- Remove lamps completely unless they are safely out of reach.

- Secure heavy furniture to the wall with bolts or with straps and brackets.

- Keep toys off the floor at night.

- Use small slide locks placed out of reach to prevent opening and closing of bifold doors that can catch fingers.

- Keep conventional doors from closing with foam doorstops that fit over the top of the door.

- Use one-piece doorjambs to eliminate the choking hazard posed by ordinary doorjambs that have removable parts. Install doorknobs without locks.

- Use bed rails.

- Don't place furniture directly under a window.

- Use a toy chest with safety hinges.

- Don't put a toy on top of a high shelf or dresser. Make the toy accessible if it's going to be in view.

- Discard anything with small parts.

a peaceful painted sky. (For an example, see page 57.) Apply blue-sky paint over a white base coat. After it dries, slap white paint over the surface using a 4-inch-wide decorator brush. Working at a 45-degree angle and making short random strokes, pull the paint out until it's thin in some areas. Overlay the paint in places for uneven color overall. Use a 2-inch-wide brush tipped in white paint to make clouds and to blend the colors. Be loose and don't think of cloud "shapes."

Above: An adorable professionally painted mural captures this toddler's favorite teddy-bear fantasy.

The labels on the bins read: BEACH WEAR, EXTRA SHEETS, CURTAINS, TSHIR[T], WINTER SHIRTS, SUMMER SHORTS, UNDERWEAR, SOCKS, CHESS

SMARTtip

Neat Storage

A well-organized closet not only makes getting dressed easier but also provides the basis for teaching the child to be orderly and to begin to take responsibility for caring for his own wardrobe and personal possessions.

1 Provide a table and chairs for your toddler where he'll eventually play games and have a snack.

2 In a small room, a bed that has a place for storage underneath can save space.

3 Bring in cute details and age-appropriate accessories that can add personality to the room.

4 Fill in with inexpensive plastic pieces that can take a beating.

5 Buy a double bed, if there is room. That way you won't have to replace the bed later.

a gallery of smart ideas

a gallery of smart ideas

1 Paint unmatched pieces of furniture the same color to coordinate them.

2 Colorful racks and pegs can be practical art on a wall. Change objects seasonally for a new look.

3 Provide a stimulating and creative environment to fuel your toddler's imagination.

4 Consider a decorating scheme that isn't age-specific. This room is perfect for ages 2 through 10.

5 Let furnishings and accessories underscore a particular decorating theme.

a gallery
of smart ideas

1 This "frontier town" is actually a facade on storage cabinet doors.

2 A "fishing tackle box" is purely decorative in a toddler's room that's designed around a weekend cabin theme.

3 Personalized items will make your toddler feel special.

4, 5, 6 Affordable plastic storage pieces can add color to the room.

7 Color-match linens to wallpaper patterns and print borders for a finished look.

William Francis

4

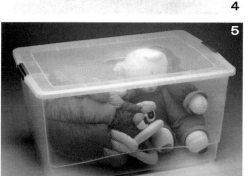

5

6

7

FURNITURE AND STORAGE

THE STORY ON STORAGE
■ **CASE GOODS** ■ **BUILT-IN FURNITURE**
■ **MODULAR SYSTEMS**
■ **FREESTANDING FURNITURE**

You can include as many elements as you like in your nursery furniture plan—depending on what comfortably fits in the room, what you can afford, and what is compatible with your overall decorating scheme. But the truth is, you don't really need a lot of furniture in the nursery. The few items that are necessary are a crib, a changing table, a rocker or glider, a chest of drawers, a side table, and a lamp. Optional items could include a clothing armoire and a toy chest. You may want to furnish the room in a way that can serve your child from his newborn months through his teens, or somewhere in the middle. All you have to do is switch the crib with a bed and change the details and accessories that quickly become too juvenile for kids as they grow. If you plan to purchase an entire suite of furniture, keep an eye on the future by planning the additional storage pieces that your child will need as time goes by, as well as a desk or computer table. A bookcase is always handy. You can use it now for stuffed animals and pictures. Later it will be handy for school books, awards, and collections of all sorts.

All of these items come in all styles, from traditional to modern. You may want to choose a style for the nursery that matches the rest of your home. On the other hand, there is no design rule that says you can't go with a

nursery that has a completely different look, a total departure from the decor in the other rooms. Even if your home is sleek and modern, there is no reason why the nursery can't be decorated in a traditional style.

Cribs, bassinets, and cradles were discussed in Chapter 2. Now here is a look at other nursery furnishings and storage options that you'll find helpful.

Below: **Some cabinets give you an opportunity to put the baby's books, toys, and other items on display.**

THE STORY ON STORAGE

In addition to providing space for clothing and extra sheets and blankets, the right storage system in a nursery starts out holding myriad precious baby needs and accessories. As the baby achieves toddlerhood, the well-designed storage space becomes an accessible, attractive place for toys and, later, for games, trinkets, and other childhood treasures. A wide array of possibilities exist, ranging from stand-alone pieces like chests, armoires, and toy boxes to built-in drawers, cubbies, and shelving (with or without doors).

CASE GOODS

Storage furniture, otherwise known as case goods, is available as built-in, modular, or freestanding units. The furniture industry uses a variety of labels to let consumers know what materials are used in a piece of case-goods furniture. The definitions of these terms are regulated by the Federal Trade Commission.

■ **Solid wood** means that the exposed surfaces are made of the specified wood, without any veneer or plywood. (You may see a label saying "solid oak" or "solid pine.") Other woods may be used on unexposed surfaces, such as the backs and sides of drawers.

■ **Genuine wood** means that all exposed parts of the furniture are made of a veneer of the wood named, over hardwood plywood.

■ **Wood** means that none of the parts of the furniture are made of plastic, metal, or other materials.

Above: **In addition to being moveable, freestanding furniture may offer as many storage options as built-in storage.**

■ **Manmade materials** refers to plastic laminate panels that are printed to look like wood. The furniture may also include plastic molded to look like wood carving or trim.

SMARTtip

What is Furniture Made Of?

Furniture can be constructed of several different wood materials:

Hardwoods, from deciduous trees such as cherry, maple, oak, ash, pecan, teak, walnut, mahogany, and poplar. These woods are often used in high-quality furniture because of their strength and durability.

Softwoods are from conifer trees, including fir, pine, redwood, cedar, and cypress. These woods must be well-seasoned and kiln-dried before lumber is used, or it will split and splinter easily.

Veneers are thin sheets of hardwood that are glued to a core of less expensive material, such as

plywood or particleboard. Veneers were once associated with poor-quality furniture, but veneer furniture made today is more acceptable and may be stronger than solid wood. Wide boards of solid wood will warp and crack with weather changes, but veneer over plywood won't.

Joining Methods To evaluate how a piece of furniture is made, look for strong construction at the joints. Most furniture is glued together or fastened with screws, or a combination of the two. Staples are often used on poor-quality pieces. Avoid these pieces, especially if they will bear weight.

BUILT-IN FURNITURE

If the nursery is oddly shaped, built-in furniture is a particularly good choice because it can be custom-made for the space. The down side is that custom-made furniture can be expensive. Before you decide whether this is the option for you, get several estimates from reputable carpenters. If you decide to go ahead with the built-in furniture, check the carpenter's references—preferably by talking to people you know and trust who have worked with the person—ask to see examples of the carpenter's work, and get the detailed estimate in writing. Make sure the estimate includes items like hardware (knobs, handles, drawer pulls, hinges, and so forth), which can create an expensive surprise if not addressed up front.

MODULAR SYSTEMS

Modular storage systems consist of separate, coordinated units that can be purchased individually or as an entire suite. Modular systems look very much like built-in furniture but, unless custom-made, are usually more affordable. The price is determined by the number of pieces and the finish that you choose. In addition, if assembly is required, you'll have to factor in that charge unless you can do the assembly yourself. To determine whether this is feasible, ask the salesperson what level of skills you'll need and what tools are required.

Top: Storage shelves create a built-in look around a mural. Use baskets to contain clutter.

Left: Many modular furniture systems allow you to create your own storage design by combining a number of individual pieces.

Opposite: Pick pieces that serve more than one function, such as this combination changing table and chest of drawers.

Ideally, this type of furniture should be purchased after you've seen it in a showroom. Check for sturdiness, and make sure that hinges and supports are strong. Run your hands across the finish to make sure that it's smooth. Inspect it for sharp corners and edges; choose pieces with rounded corners whenever possible. Shelving should be strong and adjustable so that you can install it at a safe and comfortable height for your child and then change it as

your child grows. Avoid anything with glass doors. Glass that can shatter is a safety hazard, of course, but even if the glass is shatterproof, it's not a good idea for a little one's room. Keeping a child's room clean is a tough enough job without the need for frequently wiping finger-smudged glass. Consider removing the doors or replacing glass with screening. Of course, these things don't matter when your child is newborn, but they will become important soon.

FREESTANDING FURNITURE

Dressers and chests are usually classified by how much they can hold. From smallest to largest are the lingerie chest, the drawer chest, the door chest, and the armoire (also called a wardrobe). The first two types have only drawers, whereas the door chest has drawers at the bottom and two doors at the top. The armoire has a clothes rod inside. A small dresser is the bare minimum requirement for a nursery, but as your child grows, so will her clothing storage needs. If you can—and if current space permits—get a large dresser or armoire that will be a better long-term investment.

You may want to hold off purchasing an expensive dresser until your child is a little older. You'll still need a place to store the baby's clothes, however, so consider the temporary solution of using a hand-me-down or garage-sale purchase that can be refurbished. If you decide to go the second-hand route, here are some points to remember:

■ Shake it. The furniture's construction should be solid. (See the Smart Tip on page 87.)

■ Run your hands over it. The finish should be smooth and paint should not be chipped. Otherwise, be prepared to sand, prime, and refinish it.

■ Pull out the drawers to make sure the runners are intact. If the drawers are sticky, the runners can be lubricated, but if the runners are broken, the drawers won't work properly unless you make repairs.

Remember that if repairs are in order, the purchase price and refurbishing costs of a piece of old or used furniture can add up to more than the cost of a new dresser unless you can do the work yourself.

If you're buying a new dresser, bring a measuring tape with you. You will want to make sure the piece fits nicely into the space you have planned for it. And don't rely on your ability to guess the depth, width, and height of the space inside drawers. New furniture is costly, so you'll want the dresser to last and be useful as your child grows. That won't happen if the drawers aren't deep and wide. Think ahead, and remember the "four-to-one rule": it takes four items of infant-size clothing to fill the space of an average-size 10-year-old's sweatshirt.

Once you've considered all of these options, you're almost ready to create your storage system. Before you go shopping, though, remember that no matter how much storage space you have, it never hurts to have just a bit more. Even if the nursery is small, you can create more storage space by using imagination. See the Smart Steps on the next page.

Opposite: This is a refurbished media cabinet. Note the sliding shelf under the hanging clothes and the way the doors fold out of sight.

Center: A dresser is a must for a baby's room. As your child grows you will need a large chest of drawers.

Above: Bedside tables should have rounded corners and open spaces for books and other items.

FINDING MORE STORAGE

ONE Let storage out of the closet.
A closet, cabinet, or chest isn't the only place for clothes storage. Consider pegged racks or an old coat tree that you can paint to match the room. Adorable items such as little hats and dresses are too precious to stow away. Keep them on display.

TWO Identify unused storage spaces. Pour a cup of tea, sit in a comfortable chair, and take a long look at the room. You'll undoubtedly see storage areas you wouldn't have considered before. Storage zones can lurk in corners, under eaves, on walls, and in front of the crib. Also, the closet in the nursery is the perfect space-waster: think about how you can use the space beneath all those little outfits hanging on the rod. Stack baskets or plastic containers filled with extra clothes, diapers, or baby linens on the closet floor, or install a low pole that will be reachable for your child as he gets old enough to hang up clothes.

THREE Think outside of the storage box. A box isn't the only place to store things, and often isn't the most space-efficient storage solution. For example, wicker baskets provide enormous decorative and practical versatility. Other kinds of items specifically designed for a variety of storage needs include rolling carts and freestanding and wall-mounted shelving units. Such items are manufactured in an array of sizes, shapes, colors, and materials. You can get ideas from catalogs, on-line, or at stores where these products are sold. Some items may work well as is, while others will work better after some decorative modifications, such as painting or some type of covering. And don't limit your

Top: Pegs and wall-hung hooks increase storage space without taking up valuable floor space. Make sure the fasteners you use can support the weight hanging from the pegs.

Left: Furniture outfitted with rubber tubs that slide in tracks are great for toy storage. They can take a lot of abuse without showing much wear and tear.

Opposite: Don't waste door space. These hanging pockets are inexpensive and handy for all kinds of small stuff.

thinking to containers designed specifically for storage. With a little creativity on your part, any container may work for your specific needs. Crafts stores sell hat boxes and band boxes in a variety of sizes ready for painting, decoupaging, or covering in fabric or left-over wallpaper to match the nursery's decor. The same treatment can be given to vintage suitcases, which can be stacked. Once you start

thinking in creative ways, you can find any number of unusual and unique ideas that will be both practical and decorative. In addition to new items, consider the treasures you can uncover at flea markets, yard sales, thrift stores, and recycling centers, where you're likely to find vintage trunks, toy chests, credenzas, and china cabinets that you can clean up and reclaim for the nursery.

THE CHANGING TABLE

Changing diapers will be a part of your daily routine for the first two or three years, so the right changing table is essential to make that process comfortable for you and safe for your baby. The most efficient changing table is one that allows the baby to face you as you change her; it's better for both of you. Whatever the design, the changing table should have a pad, guardrails and safety straps. If the changing table, or a dresser that you are using as such, does not come with safety straps or a pad, buy those separately and install them before using the table. Always keep the baby restrained when you're using a changing table.

Most changing tables come with either drawers or shelves underneath for storing diapers, lotion, cloth towels, and other necessities, as well as clothes. It's a good idea to have a small supply of diapers, lotion, and wipes at hand so that you won't have to take your eyes and hands off the baby when reaching for them. (See Chapter 8, "Accessories and Necessities," starting on page 146.)

Above: Changing tables often come with a shelf for storing small supplies of diapers, lotions, powder, and the like. A drawer or another shelf can hold additional items.

Opposite: Baskets help make the open shelves of this changing table more efficient. Note the guard rails for added safety. Never leave a baby unattended on a changing table.

SMARTtip   Essential Nursery Furnishings and Accessories Checklist

There are many expenses associated with putting together a nursery, and furniture and accessories account for only one part of the budget. Fortunately, the absolute necessities are few. Start with these basics, and fill in later with those things you discover will make it easier and more comfortable for you to care for your baby.

- Crib
- Changing Table
- Comfortable Chair, Rocker, or Glider
- Chest of Drawers
- Side Table
- General Lighting
- Flooring
- Table Lamp
- Mobile
- Baby Monitor

Another alternative to purchasing a changing table is to place a portable crib on top of a dresser and use it as a changing station as long as it's needed. Later, the portable crib can be removed and replaced with a hutch or a mirror.

A Chair. When you sit in the nursery to feed or hold your baby, you'll want it to be in a comfortable, cozy chair. Because most babies find the sensation of motion soothing, a rocker or glider is an ideal choice.

A Table. You'll want a small table on which you can place a lamp, perhaps the baby monitor, and maybe a soothing cup of tea to enjoy while you rock your baby to sleep.

ACCESSORIES

Most accessories are optional, but you'll want to have two essential items: a mobile over the crib and a baby monitor. Newborns are highly sensitive to visual stimulation that is combined with movement. A mobile, particularly a colorful one that also plays music, will be stimulating and entertaining to your baby. A monitor allows you to listen to your baby when you're in another room. (See Chapter 8 for more information on monitors and other accessories.)

Opposite: Using painted furniture that matches the walls helps the room appear larger than it is.

Right: A colorful mobile will stimulate your baby.

a gallery of

1 A chest with open shelving at the top comes in handy for handling the stuffed animal overflow.

2 There are many baby products available, but don't forget the simple elegance of a well-made bureau and mirror.

3 Increase storage in a small room by using wall-hung storage options.

4 Select baby-room furniture that is durable and easy to clean.

5 Choose a changing table that will be pleasant for the baby and comfortable for you to use.

6 Curtains hide the baby supplies usually found around a changing table.

7 Plan to store some of the baby's favorite things near the crib or bassinet.

smart ideas

7

1

a gallery
of smart ideas

1 Shop for furniture wisely. Veneers and laminates on cabinets and chests should be well joined to the base area. Drawers and doors should move smoothly, and hinges and hardware should be strong and secure.

2 A toy box can be convenient. If you buy one with a hinge, test it out firsthand. The hinge should be strong enough to hold the lid open for safety.

3 A wicker changing table can be used as a desk or dressing table by your child as she gets older.

4 Built-in furniture can be customized to suit the nursery's physical space as well as your storage needs.

a gallery of smart ideas

1 Corners and edges should be rounded for your baby's safety.

2 An inexpensive shelf can hold a display that can change as your baby matures.

3 A toy hammock attaches to the wall in any corner of the room.

4 Include a table or dresser lamp for soft incandescent illumination.

5 A changing table that keeps diapering supplies handy is best.

6 Don't forget this classic piece of furniture, a pint-size rocking chair.

CHAPTER 6

WALL AND WINDOW TREATMENTS

CREATIVE WAYS WITH WALLS
■ SHOPPING FOR MATERIALS
■ WINDOW TREATMENTS
■ PLANNING YOUR APPROACH

The right choices for window and wall treatments can work in tandem to pull together the look and feeling you want to create for your baby's room. They can set the tone or establish the theme for the overall design. Window and wall treatments also offer an excellent opportunity to add personality to the room by introducing color and pattern to the decor with subtle or lively hues and prints. You can create an adorable nursery in practically any room in the house with a relatively small investment in time and materials. If your funds are limited, you can still find a wide selection of affordable, fashionable soft treatments (curtains and fabric shades) and hard treatments (blinds and shutters) that come in standard sizes and are ready for installation. A couple of gallons of paint or even some types of wallcoverings and borders are not expensive, either. Choose classic themes and colors if you don't want the room to look out of style in a year or two, and try to limit cartoon or toy-inspired motifs, which are fads that become dated quickly. You may also want to avoid making the room look gender-specific. Keep all of that in mind, but remember: it's still your baby's nursery. In the end, how you decorate it and the colors and themes you choose for it should be the very best ones that you deem appropriate for the space and in keeping with your idea of a picture-perfect place for your baby. Let this chapter inspire your endeavors.

CREATIVE WAYS WITH WALLS

Before deciding on wallpaper or paint, look at the style of the furniture you plan to use in the baby's room. Is it structly functional, a bit whimsical, or a mixed bag of styles? If it's highly decorative on its own, use a palette of subtle colors and soft patterns, which will let the walls serve as a backdrop that won't compete. On the other hand, bold patterns and prints can create the personality and visual interest that boring or plain furnishings may lack. In some instances, the furniture in a baby's room is sparse or a collection of mismatched hand-me-downs. That's okay. Creating an attractive cohesive backdrop for a diverse mix of styles or "filling up the space" with a pretty wallcovering or a lively motif or even spectacular color can make up for anything that may be lacking. Here's how.

PAINT IT

A fresh coat of paint is generally the least expensive way to make a room look clean and up to date. Paint is also a versatile medium to which you can add decorative touches, such as a stenciled design or special effects such as painted plaids or stripes. Even if you're interested in just a standard paint job, applying a wonderful color to the walls will go a long way in making the room special. If you're unsure about choosing a color, see Chapter 2, "Color Their World," beginning on page 32. Color is a personal, somewhat instinctive choice, but a little bit of knowledge about how various colors "feel," what they suggest, and how colors work alone and in combination will help you develop your baby's nursery scheme.

If you're decorating with a view toward toddlerhood and a few years beyond, remember that several manufacturers now formulate and market paint products specifically for children's rooms, including glow-in-the-dark and glittery top coats, and blackboard paint that turns a surface into a chalkboard on which a child can write or draw and then erase. Some of these products don't require high-level skills for use, but other designer and specialty paints must be applied with special tools and require a level of expertise beyond what the novice can accomplish successfully. Also, check to make sure the paints are safe for the baby.

SMARTtip   Estimating Paint Needs

Don't get caught short. To estimate your paint needs, first find out the room's square footage: multiply the length of the room by the width *in feet*. Next, adjust the total square footage by subtracting 21 square feet for each standard door, 15 square feet for each standard window, and the actual square feet of any built-in feature, such as a bookcase. Paints usually specify coverage of 350 to 400 square feet per gallon, but most experts will advise planning on coverage of 300 square feet per gallon and 75 square feet per quart. With this in mind, you should always buy about 10 percent more paint than you think you'll use. So, multiply the adjusted square footage by 0.10; add that number; and then round up to the next highest quart.

Accents. One easy way to go is with a stenciled accent border that you can apply at the top of the wall or midway to create a chair-rail effect. You can purchase a ready-made template, acrylic paint, and brushes from a crafts store for a small investment. There are many appropriate designs for a nursery that range from hearts and flowers to bunny rabbits and bears. If you're a novice, stick with something simple.

Murals. A mural is a project that usually requires more skill than simple

Opposite, top: Subtle colors and simple patterns can support the design.

Opposite, bottom: A cute wall mural can make the baby's room special.

Top: Paint inch and foot markings on the wall to chart your baby's growth.

Right: Manufacturers now make paints formulated just for children's rooms.

stenciling. It can be time consuming and complex. But if you don't consider yourself an artist, you can hire either a professional or a student from a local art school to paint one in the room. If you're slightly confident about trying your hand at a mural, start with a relatively easy mural stencil kit from a crafts store.

ADD PERSONALITY WITH A WALLCOVERING

Before going any further, you should know that the term "wallpaper" is often used interchangeably with "wallcovering," even when the material has no or very little paper in it. Several types of wallcovering are available, and they come in an array of prints, patterns, colors, and themes. Popular patterns for the baby's room include ones based on nursery rhymes, animals, and alphabet-number motifs. Some patterns coordinate with fabrics for window treatments, bedding, rugs, and other decorative accessories for the room. It's also practical to choose a wallcovering that is marked washable and scrubbable.

The most popular wallcoverings for children's rooms are vinyl because the material is durable and can take a beating. You have the option of choosing between types.

Paper-backed vinyl. Most wallpaper patterns designed for nurseries and children's rooms are printed on paper-backed vinyl, which is washable and peelable. This latter feature is particularly desirable because it can be easily removed when it's time to update the room. Another attractive feature of paper-backed vinyl is that it is frequently sold prepasted, so it's easier to install.

Fabric-backed vinyl. A wallcovering that stands up well to scrubbing crayon or other tough marks, fabric-backed vinyl is made of a vinyl top layer over fiberglass or cloth. This type of wallcovering is heavier than paper-backed vinyl, but it doesn't come prepasted.

Vinyl-coated paper. Less expensive and not as durable as the other two options, vinyl-coated paper can be permanently marred by a peanut-butter handprint, for example.

Top: Here's an imaginative wall treatment. Items attached to the wall appear to be part of the wallcovering.

Left: Wallpapers come in a variety of distinctive designs. Or you can paint or hire someone to paint a mural on the wall.

Opposite: Washable and peelable vinyl wallpaper is the best choice for the nursery.

To estimate your needs, determine the room's size in square feet (length X width). Then, just as with estimating paint needs, subtract 21 square feet for each standard-size door, 15 square feet for each standard-size window, and the actual square footage of any built-in feature. This is the *adjusted square footage*, which you will divide by 30 to account for wastage from the 36 square feet in a standard roll of wallcovering. Round up to the nearest whole number. For anything other than a standard roll, ask a salesperson for help.

Before you hit the stores and begin thumbing through sample books, you may also want to review the design basics discussed in Chapter 3, "Plans and Schemes,"on page 46. In general, naturalistic patterns—floral or other nature designs—and stylized (repeated motifs) patterns go well with either traditional or casual, contemporary decorating styles. Abstracts and geometrics also complement contemporary designs. Plaids and stripes can coordinate with almost decor, and they aren't gender-specific.

Wallpaper Patterns. There are easy guidelines to keep in mind for optimal results. First, be careful about using very large patterns, which can overpower a small room. On the other hand, a tiny pattern in a large room will seem to fade away.

If the nursery will be small, you can keep it from feeling cramped by using light or neutral-color backgrounds. Alternatively, if the space is large and sparsely furnished, make it cozy with wallpaper that has a deeper background color. Some patterns come in reverse or complementary versions, so think about creatively setting off special areas, such as alcoves or eaves, or even one wall by pairing these prints.

Opposite: If you pick a solid color for the room's background, introduce pattern with accessories and fabrics.

Right: Light backgrounds on wallpaper give off an open, airy feeling and make the room seem larger.

The Economics of Paint

Painting is the least-expensive way to add color and personality to the walls, but only if you shop wisely and remember some basic points.

Paint grades. Don't skimp. Better-quality paints tend to cost more, but don't count out the high-grade products. Low-cost (and, usually, lower-quality) paints are not always a bargain. Usually they don't provide the coverage that a higher-quality paint does, so you often have to use additional coats. The extra gallons you'll buy will eat up those savings quickly.

Custom colors. From the point of view of the finished product, nothing compares with the professional look of an exact match. Even slight variations in the tone or shade of a color can clash. You'll spend more for custom colors, but they are worth it.

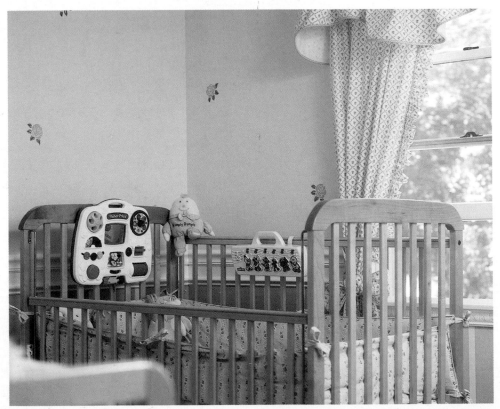

Paint Finish. Paint with a flat (nonreflective) finish is usually fine, but it won't hold up in a child's room. Unless you plan to repaint the room often, consider investing in paint with one of these finishes: *eggshell* (has a slight sheen); *satin* (has a bit more luster;) *semigloss* (is slightly glossy and is light reflective); or *gloss* (produces a hard, shiny finish). These finishes are more expensive than flat paints, but they are easier to clean with a damp cloth and mild detergent. Always be sure any paint you buy is washable.

Top: A satin finish is slightly light reflective but not shiny.

Left: Stencils are easy to apply over a solid-color wall.

Estimating Wallpaper Needs

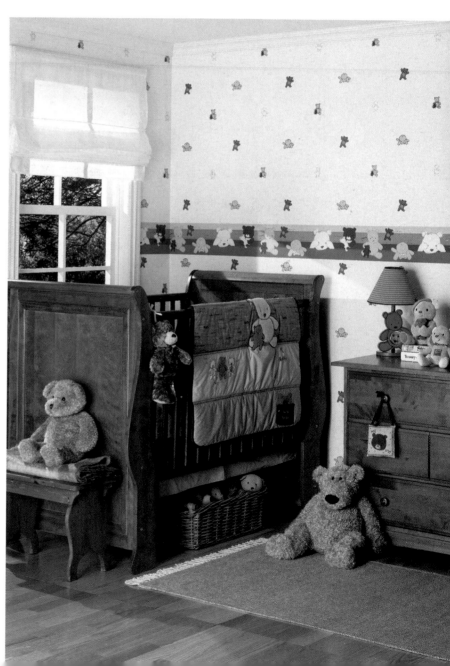

You'll want to be sure that the pattern and color you've selected are right for your baby's nursery. To "try on" a wall-covering before purchasing it; ask whether you can bring the sample book home or whether the store will give you a small cutting. An alternative is to buy one roll. Look at the pattern and colors in the room under different conditions: at different times during daylight hours, and with the lights on and off during the day and at night.

Below: **Choose a quality paint product that will last as the nursery gradually becomes the toddler's room.**

If you'd like to mix patterns but feel somewhat skittish about it, look for products by manufacturers that offer coordinated lines. Most wallpaper sample books make suggestions about patterns that mix easily. Very often, you can also purchase coordinated fabric from the same company. If you're comfortable mixing and matching on your own, don't rely solely on your educated eye. Get samples, and try them out together at home. Stick to the same colorways, and use patterns of different weights—small-, medium-, and large-scale prints, reserving the largest motif for accents, such as a ruffled valance or a dust ruffle.

SHOPPING FOR MATERIALS

SMART steps

ONE Evaluate the room's architectural features. If a painting didn't interest you, you'd quickly grow tired of having to look at it every day. The same is true of the walls of a room. If they create one big boring box, you can add architectural interest easily with inexpensive crown molding or wainscoting.

TWO Make a sketch of each wall. Before investing time and money in the project, get a better idea of how the finished wall treatments will look by making a drawing of each wall. (Follow the same directions outlined for drawing a floor plan on page 50 of Chapter 3.) Draw the dimensions of the wall to scale, including closets and windows. Make several blank photocopies of these drawings so that you can try different effects. These sketches will also be helpful when you consider window treatments.

THREE Decorate for the long term. Wallpaper with a juvenile motif may be perfect right now for the nursery, but as your child matures, will you be willing to remove the wallcovering and redecorate any time soon? If not, think about reserving any nursery-specific themes for a wallpaper border, something that is easier to remove and less costly to replace. Other options that will save redecorating time and dollars later include installing a strip of chair-rail molding one-third of the way up the wall. Then paint the portion above the chair rail a solid color, and apply wallpaper, another solid color, or a painted effect to the wall below it.

Above: Use molding and paint to create faux wainscot.

Left: Highlight the distinctive architecture in the room.

Opposite: Use borders to enliven a room's design.

FOUR Put a plan on paper. Once you've decided how you'll use wallpaper, paint, or both, measure the areas and mark the measurements in the appropriate areas on your drawings. Take these with you when you shop for your materials, so you'll have a handy reference to ensure that you'll buy the right quantities.

FIVE Create a sample board. Professional designers use sample boards all the time because they provide the opportunity to see how various colors, textures, and prints might look when they are used together in the room. A sample board costs very little to make, and it can save you the time and frustration of buying items only to have to return them. What's worse, custom-mixed paints and special wallpapers may not be returnable. (See the Smart Tip below to learn how to create a sample board.) You can take a sample board with you to shop for other items, as well.

SMARTtip

Sample Board Strategies

Use white foam-core presentation board that's sold in art-supply stores. One that measures $8\frac{1}{2}$ x 11 inches is ideal for the job. Glue swatches of fabric, paint-color chips, and wallpaper samples to it. Designate about two-thirds of the board for the wall and window treatments, and divide the remaining third between the furnishings, including the crib linens, and the flooring, including area rugs.

Remove and replace swatches and samples as you experiment with different looks, prints, and colors. Review the sample board at different times of the day, under various light conditions.

Pick one main paint color, and get a sample of it in every tone and shade you can find.

Remember, professionals get a lot of their ideas through trial and error.

WINDOW TREATMENTS

Window treatments serve numerous important functions. First, they can be used to play up attractive windows and views. They can also camouflage what you *don't* want to see, such as your neighbor's yard or the fact that the windows are shaped oddly or poorly proportioned. Second, window treatments allow you to introduce more color and pattern into the room, and help tie together a strong theme brought in by other elements, such as wallpaper and flooring. Conversely, some designs or prints can set the style and tone in the room.

Some types of window treatments will let you control the amount of natural light and air that enters the baby's room. In addition, depending on how they are constructed, some styles and materials can provide insulation. Most people need window treatments that are versatile, allowing in or closing off the outdoors only when desired.

WHAT'S IN STORE FOR YOU

It's usually a good idea to determine your overall color scheme as well as wall and ceiling finishes and floor coverings before making any final decisions about window treatments. Ideally, window treatments should complement the room by tying together all of the other decorative elements.

For the most versatility, consider combining or layering two or more of types of treatments. For example, you could combine soft, sheer curtains, which simply diffuse natural light, with lined, adjustable panels or room-darkening shades. That way the nursery can be cheerful and airy or dim and cozy depending the baby's need for play or sleep.

Another versatile design combines a soft treatment, such as a valance or swag, with blinds or shutters.

Top: Choose window shade fabric that complements the color scheme in the rest of the room.

Left: Blinds and sheer curtains and valances make a good window treatment combination. The blinds provide privacy, while the sheers allow light to filter into the room.

Cordless blinds, shades, and curtains or drapes are considered the safest types of window treatments for little ones' rooms and, in fact, in any room in which small children will spend a lot of time. Over the past decade, the window-covering industry has developed a wide range of attractive alternatives to the older cord-operated products. Innovations include cordless horizontal and vertical blinds, pleated shades, fabric roll-up shades, and wood blinds operated with a remote control device. For more information on this topic, see Chapter 9, "Safe in Any Room," beginning on page 162.

If your windows are standard sizes, you can purchase almost any type of treatment, ready for installation. Custom-ordered designs can be considerably more expensive, but they can be fitted to a nonstandard window's specifications or made to match fabrics or wallpaper patterns.

Curtains and Valances. The easiest fabrics to maintain are blends of cotton and a synthetic, typically polyester. They're washable, require little or no ironing, and are fade-resistant. If your baby has allergies or a sensitivity to fabric sizing or synthetics, an all-natural fabric is a better choice. If the windows in the nursery get lots of solar exposure, cotton curtains will fade unless they're lined.

There are many variations of these types of treatments for your consideration. One or more may be right for the nursery you are designing and the size and shape of the windows. These include panels that are short, long, ruffled, or plain; sheer or solid fabrics in tab-top, pleated, or gathered headings; and swagged, pouffed, ballooned, or festooned valances. Generally, ruffles, poufs, and other elaborate designs usually look best in traditional and country interiors, while tailored or simple window treatments can be fine anywhere, even in rooms with contemporary styling.

Top: For a baby's room, or any child's room, choose washable curtains made of cotton or a cotton-and-polyester blend.

Right: Generally, simple window treatments look best in the nursery. The straightforward design shown here works well with the traditional-style windows.

Curtains can be easily coordinated with the color, pattern, or print you've chosen for the wall treatment and bedding. Also, in a nursery, where it's natural to want to create a feeling that's soft and soothing, curtains can sometimes smooth over the geometric exactness of the typical rectangular window. Lined curtains can also cut down on drafts and block out harsh sunlight, particularly in rooms with a southern exposure and no tree or shrub foliage to filter the direct rays. Just remember that curtains must be completely closed to provide these advantages. Also, curtains collect dust, and unless they're washable, professional cleaning bills are a long-term maintenance cost that you must factor into your budget.

Blinds. The main advantage of blinds is that they are an effective means of blocking out sun completely or filtering it while allowing for ventilation. Blinds are available in metal, wood, vinyl, and textured-fabric finishes, and in vertical or horizontal slats in standard, mini, or micro widths. You can choose among a wide selection of colors, and use blinds alone or paired with curtains or valances. Blinds come in standard sizes or can be made in custom sizes.

The potentially sterile appearance of a blind used alone can be softened by adding curtains or valances. One major disadvantage of blinds is that the slats tend to attract dust; regular vacuuming with the upholstery attachment (the small round brush) of a vacuum cleaner will be less of a maintenance headache than less frequent but far more awkward cleaning alternatives, such as soaking them in the tub with detergent and warm water.

Shades. The traditional style of shade is a single piece of fabric or vinyl attached to a roller and operated with a cord or a spring mechanism. Fabric shades are available in flat, gathered, or pleated styles; variations on these include Roman, balloon, and cellular shades.

Depending on the material from which the shade is made, some shades can block out the sun completely when drawn; others serve as sun filters. In addition to controlling light, shades provide privacy. A main disadvantage is that shades are difficult to clean.

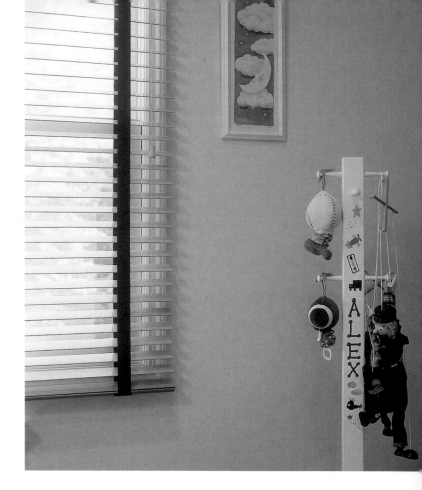

Shutters. Louvered shutters can be a versatile method of providing privacy and controlling air and light in the nursery. The panels can be opened or closed; the louvers can be adjusted to direct a breeze up or down. Shutters can be painted or stained, and some come with a panel that allows you to install fabric to match patterns and colors used on other furnishings in the room. Like blinds and shades, shutters come in a variety of standard sizes, or they can be custom-made for nonstandard or oddly shaped windows.

Typically, a contemporary design calls for wide louvers, and narrow louvers suggest a country look, but that's really more of a personal preference. Generally, shutters are installed on the bottom half of a window, with a valance or curtain panels on the top. Don't hamper your imagination and creativity, however: a number of shutter and fabric combinations look attractive together. For example, wooden louvered shutters can be paired with a pleated fabric shade, with or without a swag valance.

Opposite, top: Blinds are available in a variety of materials and a number of slat sizes.

Opposite, bottom: When closed, some cellular shades provide privacy while allowing light to filter into the room.

Above: Louvered shutters allow light and breezes into the room even when the shutters are closed. Many people install shutters on the bottom half of the window with a curtain panel on the top portion of the window. Paint the shutters to complement the room's color scheme.

SMARTtip   Windows 1, 2, 3

If your budget is tight, consider planning your window treatment so that it can be purchased and implemented in three stages. Stage one has a practical goal: control light and provide privacy. Blinds, shades, and shutters are the most obvious and effective choices to meet this need. Stage two involves adding some style that will complement the room. For this, a good-looking rod and curtain panels will serve nicely. Finally, stage three is your opportunity to add a special detail or two, such as a shaped cornice, a coordinated valance, or pretty tiebacks. Be careful, however, that your choices are safe ones for the nursery and don't contain dangling cords or objects that can harm the baby.

PLANNING YOUR APPROACH

SMART steps

ONE Look outside. If there's only one window, your task is easier. Determine whether the view out the window—and the window itself—are worth highlighting or downplaying. Fussier treatments tend to draw attention to windows, whereas simpler styles allow the attention to focus on other elements in the room instead.

TWO Note the room's orientation. The room's exposure to the sun at various times during the day will affect not only the color palette (because the way colors are perceived changes according to the light in a given space) but the function of the nursery. If one or more windows faces east, you'll need a way to block the morning's rays. A window that faces west will get afternoon sun. Windows with a northern exposure receive no direct sunlight (or warming

Opposite: Simple treatments support the rest of the room.

Left: Size the window treatment to the window.

Below: Consider the orientation of the room before choosing window treatment styles and materials.

FOUR Measure up. Don't assume that two windows in the same room have exactly the same measurements. Use a steel measuring tape, and jot down the exact dimensions of every window in the room.

FIVE Determine the price of maintenance. Custom-made treatments may be a luxury you're willing to budget for when you put the nursery together, but don't forget that some of these require professional installation and cleaning. That also means that someone has to come in to your home to remove and reinstall the treatments each time cleaning is required. Even some ready-made curtains may require professional cleaning. Delicate and special-care fabrics and trim won't stand up to machine- or hand-washing. Consider your long-term budget before deciding to go with one of these options.

rays, important in colder climates), whereas windows with a southern exposure admit direct sunlight throughout most of the day. These factors will affect how much room-darkening and insulation matter in this particular room.

THREE Select the right hardware. Will your treatment be installed inside or outside the window frame? An inside mount requires the use of a rod or pole that will fit within the window frame. For this situation, you must take accurate measurements on all of the windows. An outside mount provides more flexibility—you can use any type of hardware, and you can install it either on the window trim or directly on the wall.

Will the hardware be seen or hidden? If the hardware will be visible, make sure the style suits the decor of the room. Just as important, don't sacrifice style for function. If an installation calls for a sturdy pole, don't substitute a flimsy metal rod; the curtain won't drape properly.

1 A circus theme is a popular choice for a baby's room. Note the shape of the valance.

2 Don't forget to include personal items in your decorating. Here a child's handprint is used in two wall hangings.

3 Painting the characters from a favorite fairy tale on the wall is a popular baby's room design trend.

4 Star-shaped hooks hold up a hamper next to the changing table.

5 A stepladder is used as a display platform for toys and plants.

6 Use decorative shelves that contain pegs to increase storage while adding design interest.

a gallery of smart ideas

a gallery of smart ideas

1 A framed print carries through the theme that has been introduced in this room with the wallpaper and border.

2 A chair-rail effect is easy to achieve using a wallpaper border to divide the wall.

3 Details can add a special note. A switchplate can be painted to coordinate with a wall mural.

4 Simple curtain panels bring another palette and print into a bathroom that is part of a nursery suite.

1 Great color accentuates an alcove. The Roman shade, fabricated in plaid, will be suitable beyond the nursery years.

2 A border eases the transition from stripes on the lower half of the wall to clouds on the upper portion.

3 A subtle palette on the wall lets racy red furniture take the spotlight.

4 A swagged valance looks pretty in pink checks.

5 Nursery rhymes, such as "The Cat and the Fiddle," are always a popular theme.

a gallery of smart ideas

FLOORING FOR THE NURSERY

YOUR FLOORING OPTIONS ▪ WOOD ▪ LAMINATE PRODUCTS ▪ RESILIENT VINYL ▪ CARPETING AND RUGS

It may be hard to imagine your newborn being anywhere other than cuddled in your arms, but sooner or later your baby will be spending a lot of time on the floor, playing, sleeping, and even eating. The flooring material you choose has to be comfortable, easy to clean, and right for you and the baby. In addition, it has to work with the overall design and decor. In some cases, a colorful patterned carpet or theme rug can even be the focal point of an otherwise plain room.

Also, think of good flooring as an investment that can serve your child through toddlerhood, childhood, the teenage years, and into adulthood. However, in this chapter, you'll find information regarding various types of flooring that are particularly suitable for a nursery. (Ceramic tile would be too cold and hard, for example.)

If you're working with a professional designer, he can explain the wide range of flooring options for the room. Your designer will be able to advise you on style and about the practical considerations of what's best suited to your nursery-room needs. The choices are myriad and innovations in technology have widened the range in finishes, color-fastness, and stain-resistance. Here's how to get started.

SMART steps

ONE Measure the floor space. Draw a sketch of the room, noting entry doors, arches, built-ins, and closets. Most flooring is priced by the square foot, so measure the length and the width of the nursery in feet. Round off those figures to the next foot. Multiply these two figures to determine the square feet in the room. For example, for a room measuring 10 feet 4 inches x 12 feet 6 inches, round the fig-

ures to 11 x 13. Multiply those figures, and you'll come up with 143 square feet. That will give you extra flooring, but it is better to have a little more than less.

Some flooring, such as carpeting, is priced in square yards. To determine the number of square yards in the nursery, divide the number of square feet by 9. In our example, there are just under 16 square yards in 143 square feet.

TWO Consider your budget. Prices differ enormously for types of flooring. Even within types, there may be a broad range among different grades or qualities. For example, wool carpeting is more expensive than synthetic weaves, and top-grade wood flooring will put a much larger dent in your budget than a laminate floor. By shopping with the nursery room's dimensions (as described in Step 1), you will know right away what you can afford. Don't forget: bring your hand calculator with you.

THREE Take a field trip. Most home centers and specialty stores have excellent displays of the flooring products that they are selling, ranging from carpeting to wood, plus laminate and resilient-vinyl flooring. Pictures are worth a thousand words, and you can get ideas from TV, magazines, and the Internet. But to get a true impression of what it would be like to live with your choice, there's nothing like running your hand over the surface of a laminate sample or feeling the texture of a loop-pile rug.

FOUR Choose a complementary material. Flooring material should complement the room's design scheme. For example, in a country room, either a natural or laminate-wood floor topped with a hooked rug will supply the necessary charm.

Opposite: Babies and toddlers will play, sleep, and even eat on the floor at times, so look for carpeting or another material that is comfortable but durable and easy to clean.

Right: An old wood floor may need refinishing before the baby arrives. Fill in any cracks or spaces between the planks, and sand the wood to a smooth splinter-free finish.

YOUR FLOORING OPTIONS

Taking a comprehensive look at the types of flooring available for your baby's room ahead of time will make your job of getting the room in shape, and ready in time, easier. As you review these options, remember that some flooring materials can be mixed and matched for creative variation that allows design flexibility within every budget. However, you may want to play up or play down the colors and patterns, depending on what you've chosen for the walls.

WOOD

Wood flooring is a traditional favorite, and it is available in strips of 2 to 3 inches wide to country planks of 10 inches wide or more, or in a wide variety of other configurations

and looks. For example, the richness and visual texture of a hardwood parquet floor is a classic look that has remained popular for decades. The look of a traditional parquet floor can be had for a fraction of the cost of wood plank flooring with the prefinished hardwood tile blocks available from several manufacturers.

Should you use softwood or hardwood? Tongue-and-groove floorboards are often made out of softwoods, such as pine and fir. In contrast to the hardwoods—maple, birch, oak, or ash—softwoods are usually not a good choice for high-traffic areas. However, the softwoods usually are perfectly suitable for nurseries and older children's rooms. And remember, even though hardwoods resist becoming marred with normal use, they won't stand up to abuse.

Grades. Hardwoods and softwoods are graded according to their color, grain, and imperfections. The top of the line is known as clear, followed by select, Number 1 common, and Number 2 common. Of course, cost will have to be considered when deciding which grade of wood to use, but there are other factors to consider. For example, if you plan to sand and polyurethane the floor and leave much of it exposed, using small area rugs for accents, it's important to have the best grade you can afford. On the other hand, if you plan to install carpeting, Number 2 common is the way to go.

Stains. If you plan to stain the floor, remember that imperfections are less noticeable with darker stains. Natural wood stains range from very light ash to deep coffee tones. The lighter stains tend to make a room feel less formal, whereas the darker tones suggest a formal traditional decor. Don't forget the possibility of color stains for wood

Above: **Tap into your creativity and paint a whimsical design on a wood floor.**

floors, especially, reds, blues, and greens. Color stains suggest a casual, whimsical feel, one that may be just right for your baby's room. Lighter stains—both natural wood tones and colors—tend to make the room look larger by creating a feeling of openness. Darker stains and colors can create a cozy feeling in a large room that otherwise would seem cold.

Kits are available for do-it-yourself installations, but such projects require a fair degree of skill. For this reason, most wood-flooring installations are done by professionals.

Care. Maintaining a wood floor is easy if it has been properly sealed. Polyurethane is durable and easy to apply. Use two or three thin coats instead of one thick coat. Usually, all that's needed, then, is regular vacuuming or dust-mopping. Spots can be cleaned with products manufactured specifically for this purpose.

Above: **Protect a painted floor with an acrylic polyurethane sealer, which dries clear.**

Above, left: **A medium-tone stain will hide most minor imperfections, but it is light enough to keep the room cheerful.**

SMARTtip Look for a Bargain

Shop for a remnant carpet. You'll be surprised at the deep discount you can get from a home center or even a small store. For a minimal charge, the store will even bind the remnant to give it a finished look.

laminate flooring is a relatively quick and easy project, making it a reasonable do-it-yourself undertaking.

Care. Laminate flooring is easy to clean by vacuuming and damp-mopping (no waxing ever needed).

RESILIENT VINYL FLOORING

An option that is even easier on the budget is resilient flooring, which can be installed even by do-it-yourselfers who are not especially experienced at tackling home projects. In addition to reasonable pricing, resilient flooring is durable and easy to maintain, making it an even more attractive option for a baby's room. It can be slippery when wet, however, so you may want to place an area rug with a non-skid backing or a carpet over the surface.

Resilient flooring is manufactured in sheets and tiles, and it is available in a dazzling array of colors and patterns. With tiles, colors and patterns can be combined in an infinite number of ways to perfectly complement the rest of the vision you have created for the nursery. Tiles are fairly easy to install yourself.

LAMINATE PRODUCTS

If you crave the look of wood but question its long-term practicality in your child's room, consider a wood-floor lookalike. Laminate, also referred to as faux wood, is resistant to stains and scratches. Manufacturers offer warranties—some for up to 15 years or more—against the worst your growing child can offer, including stains, scratches, cracking, and peeling.

Laminate flooring can be applied over virtually any surface, including wood and concrete, as well as existing ceramic tile, vinyl tile, or vinyl or other sheet flooring (and even some types of carpeting). Laminate flooring may be just the ticket for the nursery budget that needs tightening. Laying

Cushioned sheet vinyl is the most resilient among this type of flooring. It's comfortable and quiet underfoot. In addition, it is stain-resistant, and the no-wax and never-wax finishes offer attractive looks that are easy to maintain.

Care. To keep vinyl and resilient flooring looking good, all you need to do is sweep it and regularly damp mop it with a light cleanser that is suitable for the material.

CARPETING AND RUGS

The sheer number of options in carpeting allows this product to meet all budget needs and all style and color preferences. For example, wall-to-wall carpeting provides a soft, warm surface for the baby to crawl on, and it offers a rich, textured look that can beautifully complement the decor of any room. The surface on which your baby will crawl, toddle, and play should be suitable for all these activities.

Carpeting is available in a vast array of material, style, color, pattern, and texture. Wool carpeting is the most durable and most expensive, but it has the advantage of being naturally fire-resistant and long-lasting. Carpeting made from synthetic fibers offers the greatest variety in color, pattern, and texture, and it is more affordable, in the short term. A good compromise that offers many of the best features of both of these types of

fibers is a wool-synthetic blend. What you'll get is a reasonably wide variety of design options, some enhanced durability, and a lower-than-pure-wool price tag.

Texture. A carpet's texture depends on the manufacturing process. The major methods are weaving, tufting, needlepunching, and flocking. Tufted carpet comes in one of three styles: cut pile (suitable for use in any room); loop pile (very durable, especially for use in high-traffic areas); and cut-and-loop pile (multicolor types being excellent at hiding soil). Woven carpet, in general, is the most durable, and flocked carpet is the least durable.

Opposite: Whitewashing old wooden plank flooring is a temporary solution that's inexpensive and charming.

Above: Carpeting with a floral trellis pattern may be pretty, but delicate, in a little girl's nursery.

Left: A tougher pile and darker hue may be a practical choice in a rough-and-ready boy's room.

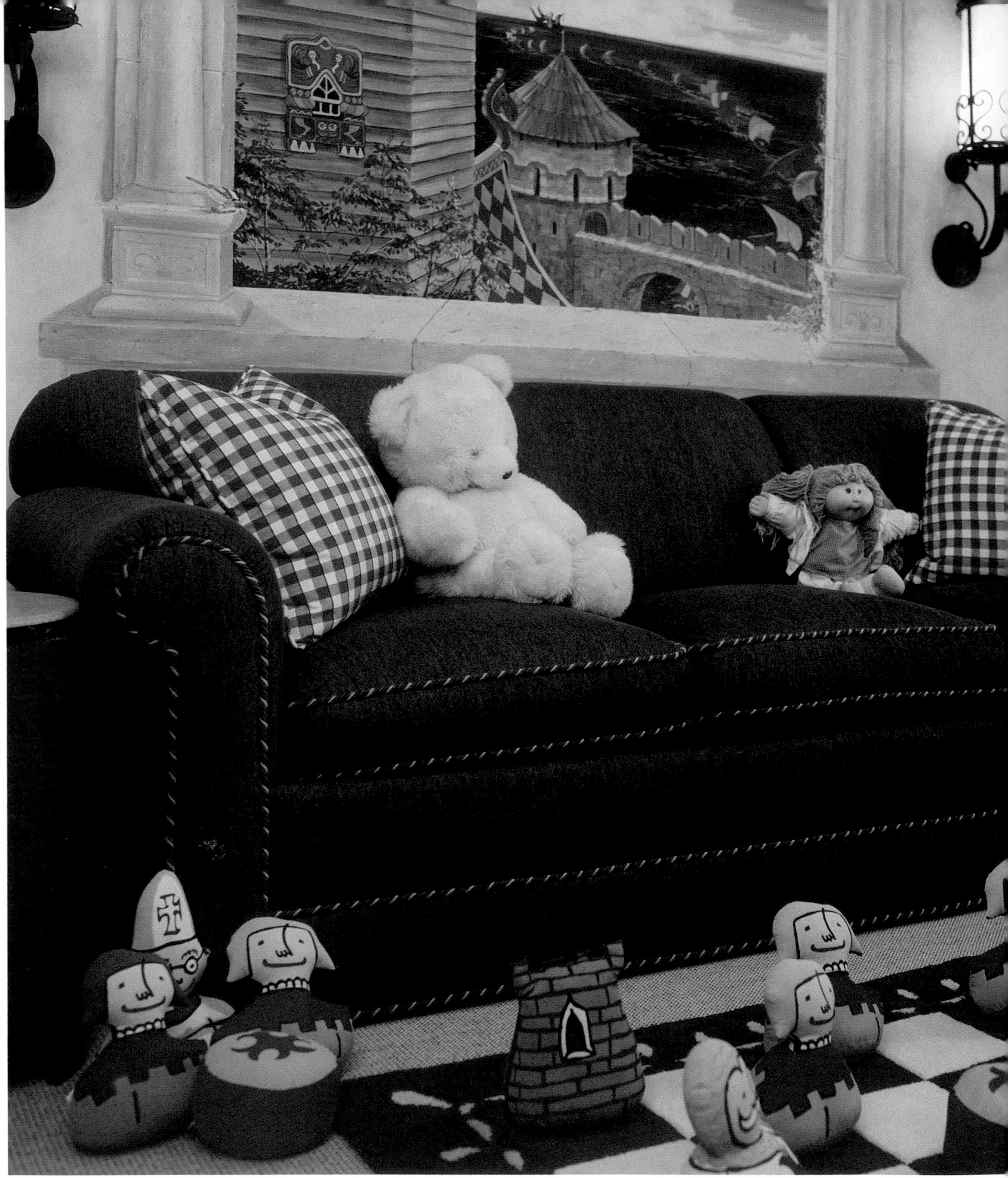

Other factors that affect the attractiveness and durability of the carpet include the type of fiber, the density and height of the pile, the thickness and quality of the yarn, and the padding installed underneath. All of these factors are important to your budget because they also affect the cost of the carpeting.

Use of area rugs is an excellent way to create separate play and sleep areas within the room or for dividing the space for, say, feeding and dressing. Area rugs also are an inexpensive way to add accent colors that help to tie the overall scheme together. For country, traditional, or period designs, an area rug can enhance the look of wood and add a touch of warmth. Hooked, braided, and rag rugs are particularly suited to rooms with a country flair. The general rule is to allow at least a foot of floor space on all four sides of the rug, creating a three-dimensional "art piece" consisting of the rug, furniture, and accessories, all set within that frame.

However, area rugs should always be backed with a nonskid material. Small rugs can be held down by attaching a hook-and-loop strip to the rug and the floor.

Carpeting and rugs are easy to maintain by regular vacuuming and, when accidents happen, prompt attention to spots and stains. It's a good investment to buy carpeting that has been treated at the mill for stain resistance.

Care. To keep most good-quality carpets fresh and looking good through years of use, clean them periodically with a steam or shampoo machine, and always clean up spills immediately. (See "Removing Carpet Stains," on the next page.)

Left: A cute "chess-board" area rug is all set for play.

Right: Wall-to-wall carpeting that has been treated at the mill for stain resistance can stand up to lots of activity.

Removing Carpet Stains

Even before the baby starts to crawl around, baby-room carpets can become soiled and stained by debris tracked in on shoes, spots from the baby oil container that was accidentally kicked onto the floor, or spills from the baby bottle that the sitter dropped. We'll take a look at some specific types of stains, but first, some general rules for removing spots and stains successfully.

1. Clean up a spot or spill immediately.
2. Use white cloths or paper towels.
3. Blot a stain—never rub or scrub.
4. Work from the outer edge in toward the center of the spot.
5. Follow up with clean water to remove any residue of the stain
6. Blot any remaining moisture by layering white paper towels over the spot and weighing them down with a heavy object.

■ **Water-Soluble Stains.** Blot as much as possible with paper towels that have been dampened in cold water. If necessary, mix a solution of ¼ teaspoon of clear, mild, nonbleach laundry detergent with one quart of water, and spray it lightly onto the spot. Blot repeatedly with white paper towels. Rinse with a spray of clean water; then blot dry.

■ **Urine or Vomit.** Mix equal parts of white vinegar and water, and blot onto the spot with white paper towels. Then, clean with detergent solution.

■ **Oil-Based Stains** (cosmetics, ink, paint, shoe polish). Blot as much as possible. Then, wearing rubber gloves to protect your hands, apply a nonflammable spot remover made specifically for grease, oil, or tar to a clean, white paper towel. Blot the stain with the treated towel.

■ **Blood, Cola, or Chocolate.** Apply a solution of 1 tablespoon of ammonia and 1 cup of water to the stain; then go over it with a detergent solution. (However, don't use ammonia on a wool carpet; instead, try an acidic stain remover, such as lemon juice or white vinegar diluted with water.)

a gallery

1 Light-painted walls can compensate for dark flooring.

2 Sometimes a rug can introduce pattern into a room.

3 If you choose a strong color, balance it against other furnishings.

4 Padding underneath the rug will make it softer underfoot and will extend the life of the carpet.

5 A laminate wood floor can be damp-mopped and will not need refinishing. It's usually guaranteed to last about 15 years.

# of smart **ideas**

5

a gallery of smart ideas

1 Always install an area rug over a bare wood floor so that there is something soft under the child's feet. Be sure the rug has a non-skid backing or mat underneath it to keep it from slipping.

2 The area rug in this room resembles ceramic tile. It adds a playful graphic element to the space, a converted-attic nursery.

3 These black-and-white "tiles" are actually painted onto old floor-boards.

a gallery of smart ideas

1 Babies don't stay in the nursery for long, so give the floors in the rest of the house some consideration, too.

2 Coordinate the room from the floor up to the ceiling. Some makers of crib linens sell matching area rugs among other accessories.

3 A cotton rug that's machine washable makes good sense.

4 Carpeting is attractive, but you'll have to vacuum it regularly to keep it looking like new.

5 A light floor keeps this nursery bright and airy looking.

6 This room's accent color was picked up from the rainbow of hues in the hooked cotton rug.

7 An adorable theme or character rug can be used as an accent in a baby or toddler's room.

5

6

7

C H A P T E R   8

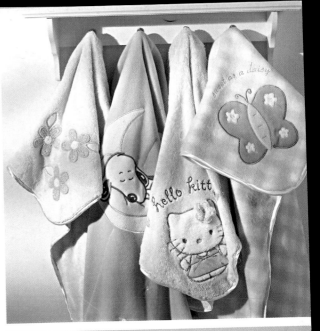

ACCESSORIES AND NECESSITIES

BABY MONITORS
■ **DIAPERS AND MORE** ■ **MOBILES AND MORE**

A few months before the birth, you'll be busy getting the nursery ready. But there is more to it than painting, putting up wallpaper, and bringing in a crib and, perhaps, a few other pieces of furniture. Besides the obvious items, there are accessories that you'll need or want for the nursery, as well. You may be shopping for these things—a baby monitor or a crib mobile—but family and friends may also want to mark the special occasion of your new arrival with gifts of their own. There are literally thousands of items for sale in baby furniture and specialty gift stores, so how do you narrow down what should go on your wish list? Aside from whatever does not specifically relate to furnishing the baby's room (a car seat or a stroller, for example) some products are great practical conveniences or time-savers in the nursery. Then, of course, there are those things that are not necessities—the accessories that will become precious keepsakes or those plain fun things for display in the nursery.

In this chapter, you'll find information about products to consider for your wish or shopping list. As with all things that you use to care for or entertain your baby, check with the Juvenile Products Manufacturers Association (JPMA), which regularly lists product recalls on their Web site. (See the Resource Guide on page 192.)

Floor Play Mat and Gym. Babies in their first year of life should always be put to sleep on their backs, but they do need "belly time" to encourage the development of the muscles and coordination that lead to crawling and walking. A washable, padded play mat provides a soft but safe surface on the floor for you to interact with your baby as you engage her in reaching for her toys and giving her exercise time to build limb strength. Just remember: it's not safe to let babies nap on their bellies on a play mat.

You may want to register at a baby specialty store or online. Whether you decide to register or not, use the following Smart Steps as a guide to developing a list of what you'll need when the baby comes, whether you receive the items as gifts or buy them yourself.

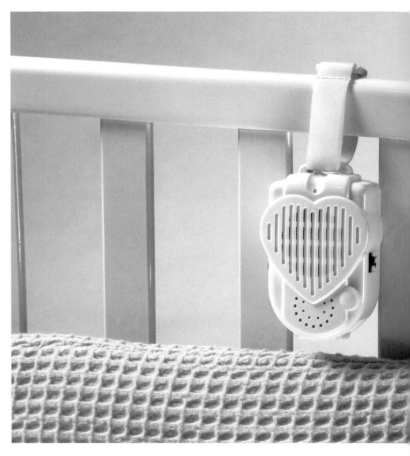

Above: A cute night light that is located away from the baby's eyes is probably safe to use. In this case, the light is plugged into an outlet near the floor and far away from the crib. A hand-painted bench adds a personal note to the room.

SMART steps

ONE List what you need first. Novelties may be adorable, but they aren't important, especially when some items are useful for only a short time. You may be able to borrow some things from relatives or friends whose kids have outgrown the need or use for an item. (Just make sure that whatever you borrow meets all of the current safety standards.)

TWO Think ahead. When you think about it, babies grow and develop at an incredibly fast pace. It seems that just when you get finished proudly reporting one milestone to friends and family, your little one achieves the next remarkable step. That's why you shouldn't stock up too much on products that your baby will outgrow—physically and developmentally—in a few short months. Prioritize your wish list, making sure to put items that you'll be able to use for many months or even several years at the top.

THREE Research and read reviews. You'll find everything you need and more on the Internet and in books and in magazines. Very often, you can find reviews for products this way, too. Always check with the JPMA to see what's on their list of recall items.

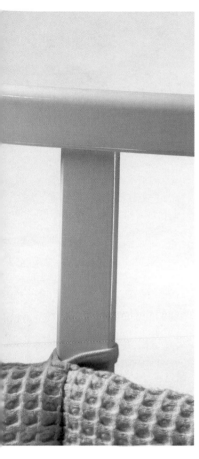

Left: This is the audio box of the product described below. It can be removed from the teddy bear housing and attached to the crib or stroller via loop-and-hook straps.

Below: This toy bear actually plays intrauterine-recorded womb sounds that lull a baby to sleep. Sound and motion sensors reactivate it.

SMARTtip   Gift Registering

More and more large stores specialize in infant and baby products, and registering has been growing among parents-to-be. The availability of on-line baby gift purchasing has helped boost the practice. Be sure to register to:

■ **Get the items and brands you want.** Gift-givers who use the registry buy exactly what's on the list. If you indicate that you want a particular brand of baby bathtub that you know is JPMA-approved for safety, you're less likely to get another style that may not be approved. When you get what you want and need, you can spend less time and energy returning or exchanging items and put more of yourself into getting ready for the baby.

■ **Get the quantities you want.** Registries let you specify that you want three of those items or two of that product. As gift-buyers check out their purchases, the items and quantities are deducted from your list, letting subsequent shoppers know what's left on your list. This prevents the bridal shower equivalent of "four toasters."

■ **Give well-wishers a range of prices.** If you choose a wide variety of items and include a good selection of inexpensive products, those buying gifts for you will be able to spend what's comfortable for them and yet know that you'll appreciate what they give you—because you chose the gift.

■ **Provide a convenient way to shop.** Many stores have an on-line shopping option so that those connected to the Internet can choose their purchases at the click of a mouse from home or the office. This is particularly nice for families and friends who live some distance away; they can purchase a gift and have it shipped. Shoppers who visit the store save time because they don't need to wander the aisles wondering what to choose.

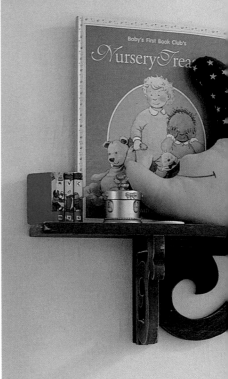

1 Baby's first toys should be soft and washable.

2 A small shelf is a versatile nursery accessory that can be used for toys or for diapering needs near the crib or changing table.

3 A playpen that you can use in the nursery and carry with you to another room is a practical accessory.

4 Include items in the baby's room that will spark his creativity.

5 Cute hats and other tiny clothing items can be displayed when not in use.

6 A baby gym comes with a mat that you can put on the nursery floor.

2

4

5

a **gallery** of smart **ideas**

3

6

a gallery of

1 A new voile canopy can dress up a refurbished antique bassinet.

2 A little coat rack can hold a small jacket or shoes.

3 Colorful toys can accessorize shelves or tables.

4 A baby carrier, also called a "Moses basket," may come with a hood or netting.

5 Bring some of your own childhood or family heirloom toys into your newborn's room.

1

2

3

4

smart **ideas**

1

a gallery of smart ideas

1 This photo grouping documents a baby's first year in frames that denote each month.

2 Bunny rabbits and garden-inspired themes have perennial cheerful appeal in a nursery.

3 If the gate goes down, this crib alarm plays soft music to alert you without waking the baby.

4 Baskets are handy for everything from toys to diapers.

5 Feel free to be creative when decorating the nursery. This playful arrangement of family photos can be easily rearranged or swapped for something else.

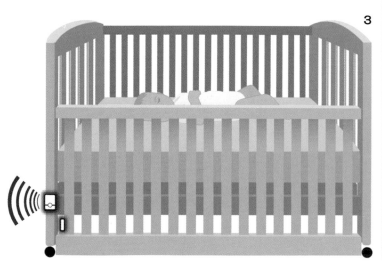

CHAPTER 9

SAFE IN ANY ROOM

SAFETY IN THE NURSERY
■ **BABY-PROOFING THE REST OF THE HOME**

Keeping your baby safe requires attention to a number of details. In this chapter, we'll consider some of the most important issues to address in the nursery and beyond. One general word of advice concerns products that would be used anywhere in the home, including the baby's room, as well as outdoors and riding in a car: before purchasing any products—either new or used—check with the Consumer Product Safety Commission (CPSC) to make sure the product has not been recalled. The contact information for the CPSC can be found in the Resource Guide, on page 192. You can also check the CPSC's Web site, which is updated monthly with new recalls.

One of the most important steps you can take to protect your baby—and your whole family—is to ensure that you have at least one smoke detector on every level of your home. (Larger homes may require more than one unit per floor.) In addition, if your home is heated with gas or oil or if you have an attached garage, carbon monoxide detectors should be placed near the bedrooms. Change the batteries in these devices according to the manufacturers' recommendations, or at least once a year. Contact your local building department to find out what you need to do to make sure your smoke detectors are up to code.

SAFETY IN THE NURSERY

If you're thinking of using a bassinet or cradle during the baby's first few months, make sure that the one you choose comes with a sturdy bottom and a wide base. If you're using a previously owned bassinet, feel the surfaces inside and outside to make sure that there are no splinters, staples, or other sources of potential cuts and scratches. If the legs fold, inspect the leg locks to determine that they are in working order and won't collapse unexpectedly while the bassinet is in use. If there are spindles, the spaces between them should be no larger than 2⅜ inch. Always use a firm new mattress that fits snugly.

When you are using a changing table, a safety strap is a must. If your changing table did not come with a strap, purchase one separately, install it, and always use it to keep the baby from falling when the table is in use. A changing table should have drawers or shelves so that diapers and other necessities (powder, wipes, lotions, and medications) will be easily accessible. You should not have to take your eyes or your hands off the baby at any time while you are changing or dressing him.

CRIB SAFETY

Some important issues about crib safety were addressed earlier in Chapter 1, "Sweet Dreams," beginning on page 12, but a number of other issues regarding products sold for babies, toddlers, and infants have to be considered. The Juvenile Products Manufacturers Association (JPMA) is an industry trade association that promotes safe products for babies and children. It's worth spending some time browsing the organization's Web site or contacting them to receive their frequently updated literature to keep current about ongoing safety concerns.

For example, the JPMA advises removing pacifiers from the crib when the baby is sleeping. The JPMA also says that it's important to keep the drop side of the crib up when the baby is inside. In addition, be careful where you place the crib when you're arranging the nursery. Cribs should never be located near windows, drapery, blinds, or anything else

Left: **You should be able to rock your baby to sleep and lock the cradle in place for safety.**

with a long cord that poses a strangulation hazard.

The National Safety Council (NSC) has advice about antique cribs. The NSC says that if a crib has decorative cut-outs, corner posts, or lead paint, get rid of it—despite the sentimental value. At least, don't use it for the baby. Keep it for decorative purposes, and use it later when you child is older and is not at any risk. The NSC also cautions against using plastic packaging materials, such as a dry-cleaning bag, for a mattress cover. "Plastic film can cling to children's faces and should never be near the crib," says the NSC.

BABY-PROOFING THE REST OF THE HOME

As your baby begins to crawl, then "furniture-walk," and finally take her first steps unaided, she will start to explore her world in new and delightful ways—not just in the nursery but throughout your home. When this happens, you'll face a new set of challenges in guarding your baby's safety. Here are some guidelines.

In the Bathroom. A baby bath seat or ring can be of great help when you're bathing the baby. For safe use, make sure that the suction cups are securely fastened to the seat or ring and that they achieve good suction on a smooth surface in the tub. These devices should be used with the tub filled only to the level at which the baby's legs are covered. Even if the baby seems

Top: A crib-rail teether is made of soft plastic that won't hurt a baby's soft gums. This device, which is FDA-approved, prevents a teething baby from ingesting varnish or paint.

Above: Baby quilts and pillows look pretty in the crib, but you should remove them to prevent a smothering hazard. Use only a thin baby blanket for an infant.

securely placed in the bath seat or ring, never leave him unattended or in the care of an older sibling.

To prevent accidental drowning in the toilet, keep the lid down and use a toilet clip.

In the Kitchen and Dining Room. Having your baby with the family in the kitchen or dining room during mealtimes can be delightful for everyone. It's an important opportunity for socialization with the baby. To be safe, a high chair should have a wide, stable base, and if it is a folding chair, the lock should be sturdy enough to prevent the chair from collapsing. High chairs should have restraining straps at the baby's waist and crotch; the straps should not be attached to the tray; and the waist strap should be easy to unclip.

Hook-on chairs have gained popularity as an alternative to free-standing high chairs. Hook-on chairs attach to the table or counter with a clamp to hold the device in place. Make sure the baby's feet can't reach any part of the table or counter, or she could dislodge the chair. The chair should have a restraining strap to hold the baby.

Around the Stairs and Landings. To keep your baby from tumbling down the stairs, safety gates are a must as soon as he starts to crawl. But make sure you use the right type of gate. One that is secured between two surfaces by a spring lock is probably fine to keep your crawler or toddler from climbing upstairs. However, you need something that is more secure at the top of the stairs. A gate that screws securely into the wall is a better choice. Whatever model you buy, make sure it is certified by the JPMA.

If the balusters on a stair railing are 5 inches or more apart, use a plastic mesh barrier to keep little ones from putting their heads through the spaces.

Around Cabinets and Drawers. Purchase inexpensive latches to prevent tots from opening cabinets and drawers where dangers lurk. In the kitchen and bathroom, this means keeping all cleaning products and medications, as well as sharp objects such as scissors and knives, from getting into the hands of your little one. In other rooms, draw-

Opposite: Every room in the house will eventually pose a safety hazard. Be sure to go through and take note of possible dangerous situations or objects.

Above: A crib tent helps to prevent a child from climbing or falling out of a crib. The airy mesh dome can be secured to the crib rails with sturdy hook-and-loop tape.

SMARTtip   Hitting the Road

While you're focusing on safety issues in the home, it's a good idea to review what's safe in your home-away-from-home: the car.

■ Babies under 1 year old and less than 20 pounds should ride in rear-facing infant or convertible car seats in the back seat. The baby should never be placed in the front seat of a car equipped with a passenger-side airbag.

■ If your baby is under 1 year old and more than 20 pounds, make sure the car seat you have is approved for his weight. He should ride facing the rear until he is at least 1 year old.

■ Babies who have passed their first birthday can ride in a forward-facing car seat.

ers and cabinets may contain household repair tools; sewing or crafts tools and supplies; home office items, such as pens and pencils; or choking hazards, such as poker chips or buttons.

Around Furniture. Always make sure that bookcases, etagères, china cabinets, and other tall objects won't come crashing down on a curious climber by securing the furniture to a wall with a strong bracket. Check all furniture for sharp corners, and install inexpensive removable bumpers.

Relating to Plants. Take a plant survey, and make sure you know whether the lush foliage or blooms decorating your home are safe or poisonous. Some plants—for example, dief-

fenbachia and poinsettia—are dangerous if they are ingested by your baby.

Electrical Outlets. Make sure sockets, outlets, and power strips are blocked with childproofing plastic caps.

Around Fireplaces and Stoves. There's no need to avoid using a wood stove or fireplace just because you have little ones in the house, but extra precautions are essential. In fact, an easily movable mesh "surround screen" or hearth gate is a good idea in a house with kids of any age. A number of designs are available to accommodate a variety of types of fireplace and stove installations. A local supplier of fireplaces, wood stoves, and accessories will be able to walk you through catalog selections or guide you to manufacturers' Web sites to help you find the right screen for your home, preferably one with a safety lock.

For stone hearths that are raised above floor level, heat-resistant, soft bumpers are available to protect children from getting hurt if they stumble and fall against the hearth.

Left: Try to make sure that furniture pieces don't have any sharp protruding corners or rough edges.

Opposite: Wicker furniture is always charming, but antique or vintage items may have loose pieces that can be ingested or scratch the baby's skin.

SAFE WINDOW TREATMENTS

Cordless blinds, shades, and drapery are considered the safest types of window treatments for little ones' rooms and, in fact, in any room in which small children will spend a lot of time. Over the past decade, the window-covering industry has developed a wide range of attractive alternatives to the older cord-operated products. Innovations include cordless horizontal and vertical blinds, pleated shades, fabric roll-up shades, and wood blinds operated with a remote control device.

Blinds and other window hangings with cords pose the risk for strangulation if the baby can reach them—toddling through the house, climbing on a bed or other furniture, or even stretching through the slats of a crib. In general, the Window Covering Safety Council (WCSC) recommends three methods of childproofing to avoid cord hazards: move cribs, beds, and all other furniture away from windows; lock cords at the head rail when blinds are lowered, and install cord stops; and secure double cords out of reach using cleats that are attached to the wall. For continuous-loop cords on vertical blinds and some draperies, use a tie-down device that is secured to the wall or floor.

In 1994, recognizing the hazard that window cords represent, the United States window-coverings industry began to redesign products for improved cord safety, with new standards implemented in 2001. If you have products in your home manufactured before 2001, they can be retrofitted with cord stops, tassels, or tie-down devices that are available free of charge from the WCSC. (See the "Resource Guide.") To date, efforts by the WCSC have resulted in the repair of millions of residential window coverings.

Window Guards. Don't count on storm windows or screens to keep tots from tumbling out of windows. For windows above ground level, window guards are a must.

Covering all the bases can be a daunting job, but it will be easier if you take a systematic approach and make a room-by-room inspection.

ONE Take a pad and pencil, and go into each room of your home. Sit where you can see the entire room—floor to ceiling. Begin with a visual survey of the walls, windows, and doors, starting from one corner. Note the potential hazards to be addressed.

TWO Look over the furniture to find any potential problems. Don't forget to examine any built-ins for doors that could be pried open or shelves that are less than sturdy.

THREE Determine whether any windows or window treatments are risky. Assess whether window guards are needed. Don't forget that even crawling babies can be surprisingly agile when it comes to climbing on furniture, and an accessible window may be a huge temptation. Inspect your window treatments to make certain your child won't be able to reach any dangling cords. (See the section on "Safe Window Treatments," page 169.)

FOUR Purchase necessary safety devices. What you buy and when you buy it depend on the specific location, the layout of your home, and the age of the baby. Unless you have already installed them, start by installing smoke and carbon monoxide detectors. As the baby grows to get to a stage where she begins to crawl, other items you may need throughout the house will include plastic caps for electrical plugs and guards for the edges of furniture and counters. And, again, depending on your home, you may

need one or more gates to keep the baby from climbing up or falling down stairs; furniture straps to secure items such as bookcases to the wall; and cabinet locks to keep curious hands out of cleaning supplies and other dangerous items.

SMARTtip   Be Alert

Babies are notorious for catching even the most organized and careful parent off guard. Here's a list of miscellaneous things to do that you may not otherwise consider.

■ Stow visitors' purses and briefcases out of reach. Babies can become entangled in straps, and strangulation is a risk. The contents of purses and other bags may present choking or poisoning hazards.

■ Clear magnets off the refrigerator, unless they're the flat, wafer-thin type that cling strongly to the surface of the appliance. Other types of decorative magnets—ceramic fruit, plastic letters, and so on—can easily be knocked off and land on the floor, posing a choking risk for babies.

■ Watch the wicker. Wicker baskets, chairs, and other decorative items start out with a tight weave, but over time wicker can dry out or become worn. Little pieces can break off and represent a choking hazard if they're pried loose by small fingers.

■ Don't let bumpers become boosters. The bumpers in a crib help keep the baby's head from injury, but once he starts to become a climber, the bumpers can allow a baby to attain enough height to tumble over the side of the crib. Remove bumpers when the baby begins to pull himself up on the crib rails.

■ Pay attention to containers of water in the home. Drownings don't just happen in pools. More than 100 children die every year from drowning in water in bathtubs, hot tubs, spas, and even toilets and buckets.

Above: Create a safe haven for your child. Remove all hazards. Use window treatments that do not have dangling cords.

2

3

5

4

a gallery of smart ideas

1 Crib bedding should be dust-, mite-, mold-, and fire-resistant.

2 Don't store anything on a low shelf that the baby can reach once she can crawl.

3 Crib heights are for the parents' comfort, but you can find ones that sit closer to the floor.

4 A foam cushion makes a changing table comfortable.

5 A baby bathtub should be elevated at one end so that water pools at the feet, not the head.

6 A crib tent keeps family pets and pests out of the crib.

6

MEETING SPECIAL NEEDS

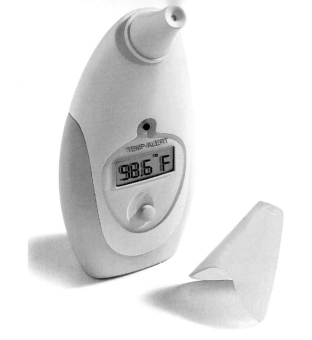

PHYSICAL DISABILITIES
■ ALLERGY AND ASTHMA ISSUES

If your baby has a medical condition or other special challenges, your entire home may have to be adapted to meet those needs. Because the nursery is where the baby will spend much of his time, your attention and effort should be spent on creating a soft, comfortable haven in which he can rest, play, and grow.

By definition, creating a nursery for any child is an exercise in planning an adapted environment. Ideally, everything that goes into the room and onto the walls and floors should be intended to enhance the baby's well-being, as well as your ability to care for her as simply as possible. If you take a long-term view, the work you do in the nursery can benefit your little one well into her toddler and grade-school years. By making some thoughtful modifications, you can adapt her room to keep it comfortable, safe, fun, stimulating, and age-appropriate, whatever challenges or health considerations she may face now or in the future. For example, storage areas for toys and even some clothing should be low enough to be accessible once she gets a little older. Furniture that has drawers or doors should have handles rather than pulls or knobs, which are sometimes difficult for little hands to grab. Most of these adaptations are common-sense adjustments. The same is true for the nursery of a special-needs child.

PHYSICAL DISABILITIES

The are different types of physical challenges that some children must face, including visual and hearing impairments, as well as mobility problems. This chapter will address some of those as they relate to nursery design.

VISUAL IMPAIRMENTS

Children with poor vision benefit from bright light but are more sensitive to glare than those with unimpaired vision, for example. Choose furniture with a matte finish, and be cautious about reflective surfaces—you'll want to re-position furniture and accessories that create glare.

Natural as opposed to artificial light is most helpful to children with visual impairments, so choose a room for the nursery that gets a lot of sunlight (but not direct sunshine). Factors such as the elevation of your home, the placement of shade trees, and the location of nearby buildings affect the amount of sunlight that reaches any given room, but usually a southeastern exposure on one wall will provide more than enough natural light. For color schemes, choose bright contrasts for interest and stimulation.

IMPAIRED MOTOR SKILLS

If your baby has a physical disability, you'll want to anticipate and continually re-assess his levels of need and ability as time passes and he grows. Here are the things to consider:

- **Fine motor skills** affect activities such as flipping light switches and turning doorknobs.
- **Upper body strength** is required to open doors and drawers.
- **Extent of reach** determines the ability to retrieve objects and control lighting in the room.
- **Stamina** affects a child's ability to open a heavy door, lift herself in and out of bed, climb stairs, or cross a room.
- **Gross motor skills** are needed to maneuver a wheelchair or walker precisely and to get around the room.

Wheelchair- and Walker-Friendly Space. If you anticipate that your baby will use a wheelchair or walker when she

Left: Furnish the bedroom with light-colored materials and matte finishes to cut down on glare.

Above: Plan ahead. Talking wall switches can be of assistance, later, to a non-verbal child.

Opposite: Experts recommend choosing a room with lots of natural light for a child with impaired vision.

Above: **Keep traffic aisles clear for children who may need assistance from a wheelchair or walker later.**

grows up, you may want to address accessibility sooner rather than later because you may have to modify the physical space. That may entail hiring a contractor to make changes in either the size of the room or the width of the doorways.

A wheelchair requires a 5-foot radius of space to turn around. Children who use walkers need sufficient clearance to maneuver, as well. Unless you plan to relocate your baby to another room, later, the nursery should be large enough so that all of the furniture and activity stations can be against the wall to keep the center of the room and the traf-

fic aisles free of any obstruction. It's also a good idea to measure the bedroom door to make sure it's large enough for the easy passage of wheelchairs and walkers. The opening should be at least 32 inches wide. If the passage is too narrow, a relatively simple fix is to reinstall the door on offset or swing-clear hinges or to install a pocket door, which slides inside the wall. If that won't solve the problem, you'll have to widen the opening.

Another potential problem with doorways is the clearance of wall space next to the door handle. At least 18 inches of clearance is necessary to grab and turn the handle or knob. Clearance problems may be solved by exchanging the door for one that can be installed in the opposite direction—that is, replace a door with a right-hand swing for one with a left-hand swing. Again, another option is a pocket door. The most costly solution is to install an automatic door that opens by remote control or that operates on sensors.

If your child will have difficulty gripping and turning knobs, replace them with lever- or loop-type hardware. Extensions are available that convert ordinary knobs into lever-type knobs. These are available in two types: one that installs permanently, and one that the child can take with him to use on any door in the house. If a child has use of only one arm, it may be necessary to reinstall doors so that the handles are accessible. If the weight of a solid-wood door is a problem, install a lightweight, hollow-core door.

A good way to test for door accessibility is the closed-fist test. If you can't open the door easily with just one hand closed into a fist, an adaptation needs to be made. (And, of course, the adaptation should pass the closed-fist test.)

In addition to these particular modifications, there are steps you can take to generally improve the nursery and, later, the maturing child's room.

 SMART steps

ONE Eliminate obstacles. In adapting the nursery, think about how you can eliminate obstacles that would keep your child dependent on others for things she can learn to do for herself. Ask your pediatrician for suggestions.

TWO Maximize areas of ability. As your child grows and develops, he will demonstrate specific skills and abilities. For example, a child who has a lower-extremity disability may have no problems when it comes to activities or tasks that call upon upper body strength. In this case, you may not need to—or want to—eliminate furniture with drawers or remove closet doors, because opening drawers and doors requires the use and flexibility of unaffected muscle groups.

THREE Seek advice. Nonprofit organizations and associations devoted to research and education on various medical conditions often are excellent resources for such information. Many sponsor parent support groups as well; parents who have children with the same special needs as yours can be a fountain of practical information that you'll get nowhere else. If you have access to the Internet, most of these groups have Web sites that are easily located through a quick search using almost any browser software.

ALLERGY AND ASTHMA ISSUES

Babies who are diagnosed with asthma or environmental allergies need a place to sleep and play that is as free as possible from agents that trigger allergic reactions and asthmatic episodes. These agents, known as allergens, include dust mites, animal dander, bits of plants and insects, mold and fungus, and fabric fragments. If your baby is diagnosed with allergies or asthma, there are several things you can do to create a more healthful environment in the nursery.

Above: An air purifier can filter out pollen, smoke, bacteria, dust, and unpleasant nursery odors. A small model can sit on the nightstand in the nursery.

ONE Seal the mattress. Cover the crib mattress in an airtight, washable plastic cover. For safety's sake, only use a well-fitting cover with a zipper. If the baby is young enough to need bumpers in the crib, use the type that come with cotton covers. Wash bedding—including bumper covers—in hot water to kill dust mites.

TWO Don't provide a home for dust. Dust collects readily in the pleats, folds, and nap of fabrics on curtains and in upholstered furniture, so keep fabric accessories to a bare minimum. In addition, seek out and eliminate other potential surfaces where dust tends to collect. For example, dusting a roller blind is easy and fast, but a mini-blind, with all those slats, may be a dusting job that you'll skip or skim on during a busy cleaning day. Also, plush toys, as soft and cuddly as they may be, can cause some disastrous attacks in sensitive children. To be on the safe side—and with the approval of your pediatrician or family doctor—keep one or two stuffed animals that are machine-washable, and wash them at least every week—with no exception.

THREE Choose a hard floor surface. Carpeting is problematic for two reasons. First, it collects dust easily and, even with diligent vacuuming, it retains dust, mites, mold and fungus spores, and debris tracked in from outside on shoes. Second, many children with allergies are sensitive to the chemicals in carpet padding. In contrast, a hardwood floor is easy to clean regularly and thoroughly.

If the floor in the nursery, or anywhere in the house, needs refinishing, it's best to leave with the baby during the process. It's important to clean the floor after sanding. If you will do the work, rent a special vacuum with a *high-efficiency particulate air* (HEPA) filtration system to remove all of the particles of dust. Choose a varnish with a low volatile organic compound (VOC) rating. Finally, make sure the windows are left open for several days before bringing your little one back into the house.

FOUR Condition the air. Children with allergies and asthma breathe easier when the air is on the dry side. They have a more difficult time when the air is hot and extremely humid. An air conditioner should be used, starting at the beginning of allergy season in the early spring. The ideal relative humidity is 30 to 50 percent, so if you live in an area where the humidity is more than your air conditioner handles, you may also need to use a dehumidifier. For children with severe allergies, a HEPA filter may be helpful.

The transitions from a hard floor surface—such as wood or tile—to carpeting can present problems for children who will be using wheelchairs or assistive devices to walk. To prevent difficulties later, consider these transition areas carefully when planning the nursery.

- Metal threshold strips should be used to prevent a bump in the flooring surface that could present a risk for tripping and falling.

- Carpeting and matting should be no thicker than $1/2$ inch.

- To protect walls from damage that can result from maneuvering a wheelchair or walker, consider running carpeting 4 or 5 inches up the wall.

Talk to your doctor about the baby's specific needs regarding air filtration and humidity control.

FIVE Manage mold. Moisture is the perfect environment for mold, and mold is a key asthma trigger. Look for both obvious and hidden sources of dampness and moisture. For example, that leaky pipe under the kitchen sink may be readily apparent, but you may not think about keeping the drip pans in the air conditioner, refrigerator, and dehumidifier clean and dry.

SIX Deal with pests. The droppings and body parts of cockroaches or rodents represent an important cause of asthma attacks. Prevent such problems by storing food in airtight containers, properly disposing of garbage, and clearing up immediately after meals. To eliminate cockroaches and rodents, first try methods other than spraying (such as poison bait or traps). If you must use pesticide spray, follow the manufacturer's instructions carefully, limit the spray to the area of infestation, and keep the baby in another room or out of the house, away from exposure.

SEVEN Keep animals away. Children with asthma or allergies may have an attack triggered by exposure to animal-skin flakes, urine, or saliva. Even if your child tolerates the presence of the family pet, it's best to keep the contact

Above, left: A hardwood floor is easy to clean, which makes it preferable for children with allergies or asthma.

Above: It's easier for a wheelchair to move from a hard floor to carpeting if the carpet pile is low.

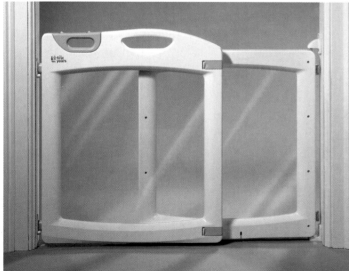

Top: An air filter on wheels can be moved to any room.

Above: A gate helps you contain your baby's environment.

Opposite: Stick to easy-to-clean surfaces.

confined to the general living areas of the house. Pets should not be allowed into the nursery, and certainly should not be permitted to roll on clean linens and clothes in the laundry room. In addition, pets should be kept away from upholstered furniture, carpeting, and area rugs.

Remember the general recommendation that "less is more" in the nursery. The fewer surfaces and fabrics there are to collect allergens, the healthier the environment will be.

EIGHT Banish smokers. Your child can have an asthma attack from exposure to smoke from a burning cigarette, cigar, or pipe, as well as the smoke exhaled by someone using these tobacco products. To protect your child, don't smoke in your home or car and don't let others do it either.

SMARTtip   Special Car Seats

Many children with special needs can ride in standard car seats with no modifications. However, according to the American Academy of Pediatrics (AAP), some medical conditions require the use of special car safety seats or restraints. Examples include breathing problems, conditions affecting muscle control, and braces or casts.

Specialized car safety seats and child restraints can be quite expensive, but in some cases, a health insurance plan (including Medicaid) may cover the cost. To find a special needs car safety seat program in your area, the following resources may be helpful:

■ Your pediatrician or family doctor

■ A nearby children's hospital

■ Your child's rehabilitation therapist

■ Easter Seals (call toll-free, 800/221-6827)

■ A Child Passenger Safety Technician, from the National Highway Traffic Safety Administration (NHTSA). (For more information, see the Resource Guide, on page 192.)

a gallery of smart ideas

1 Choose furniture that is easy to keep dust- and mold-free. Pulls are easier to handle than knobs.

2 This educational toy develops eye-hand coordination and motor skills.

3 This book appears to talk. Actually, it plays prerecorded readings that you can make for your baby.

4 Little hands can easily maneuver the door, drawer, and lid on this storage box.

5, 6, 7 Specially adapted toys may come with large, easy-to-use switches so that a physically impaired child can operate them without help.

APPENDIX: BABY ROOMS TEMPLATES

Window and Door Templates

Windows

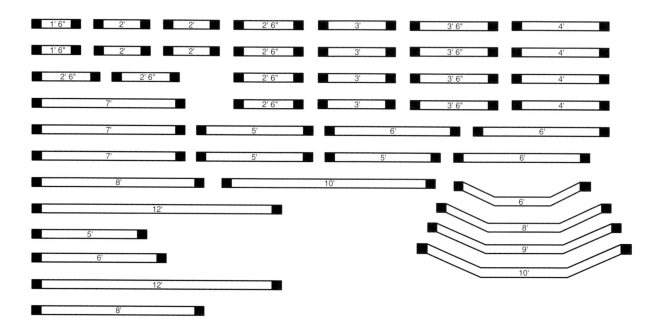

Doors

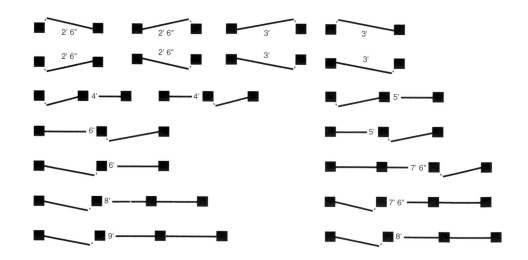

Appendix: Furniture Templates

Beds

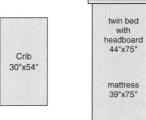

Crib
30"x54"

twin bed
with
headboard
44"x75"

mattress
39"x75"

double bed
with
headboard
59"x75"

mattress
54"x75"

queen size
with
headboard
64"x80"

mattress
60"x80"

king size
with
headboard
83"x80"

mattress
78"x80"

Case Goods

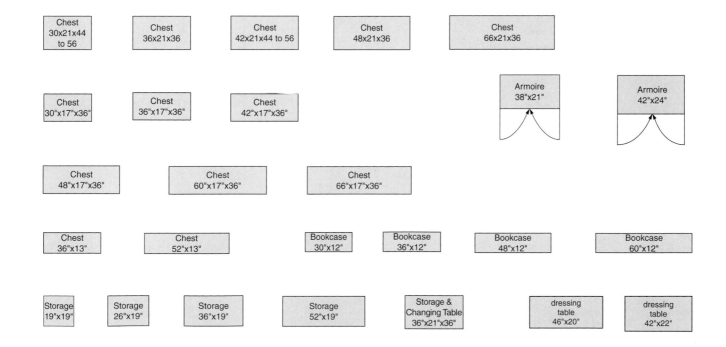

Chest
30x21x44
to 56

Chest
36x21x36

Chest
42x21x44 to 56

Chest
48x21x36

Chest
66x21x36

Chest
30"x17"x36"

Chest
36"x17"x36"

Chest
42"x17"x36"

Armoire
38"x21"

Armoire
42"x24"

Chest
48"x17"x36"

Chest
60"x17"x36"

Chest
66"x17"x36"

Chest
36"x13"

Chest
52"x13"

Bookcase
30"x12"

Bookcase
36"x12"

Bookcase
48"x12"

Bookcase
60"x12"

Storage
19"x19"

Storage
26"x19"

Storage
36"x19"

Storage
52"x19"

Storage &
Changing Table
36"x21"x36"

dressing
table
46"x20"

dressing
table
42"x22"

Appendix: Furniture Templates

Built-In Cabinets

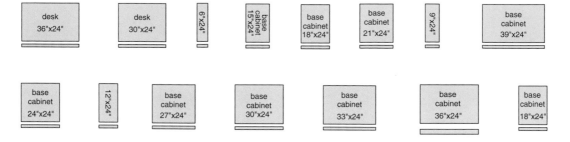

Tables and Desks

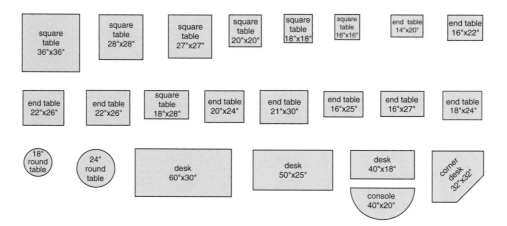

Chairs and Ottomans

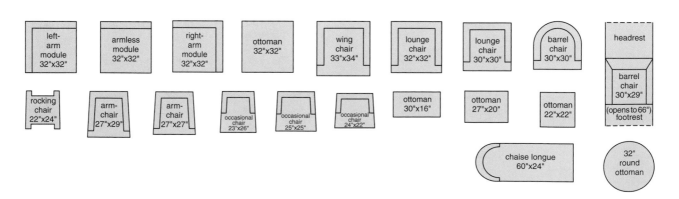

Appendix: Furniture Templates

Sofas, Love Seats, and Sofa Beds

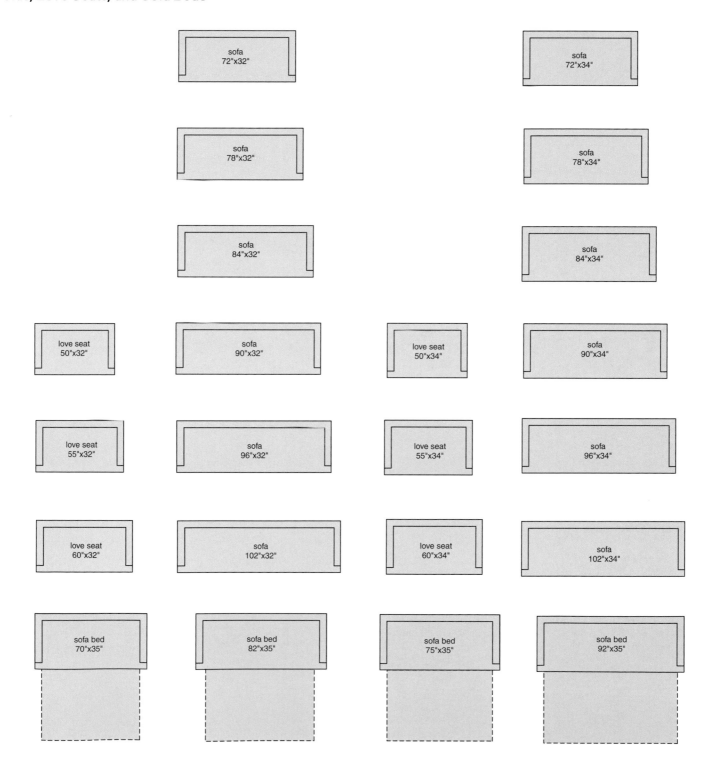

RESOURCE GUIDE

The following list of manufacturers and associations is meant to be a general guide to additional industry and product-related sources. It is not intended as a listing of products and manufacturers represented by the photographs in this book.

ASSOCIATIONS

American Academy of Pediatrics (AAP)
is a national organization of pediatric health providers with information for parents and a referral service.
141 Northwest Point Blvd.
Elk Grove Village, IL 60007-1098
Phone: 847-434-4000
www.aap.org

American Association of Poison Control Centers (AAPCC) *is a national organization that provides listings of local poison-control centers.*
3201 New Mexico Ave., Ste. 330
Washington, DC 20016
Phone: 202-362-7217
www.aapcc.org
In case of poisoning emergencies, call:
800-222-1222

American Sudden Infant Death Syndrome (SIDS) Institute *provides related information.*
2480 Windy Hill Rd., Ste. 380
Marietta, GA 30067
Phone: 800-232-7437
www.sids.org

Better Sleep Council (BSC) *provides related consumer information.*
333 Commerce St.
Alexandria, VA 22314
Phone: 703-683-8371
www.bettersleep.org

Consumer Product Safety Commission (CPSC)
is an independent federal regulatory agency that offers information about products and safety recalls.
Phone: 800-638-2772
www.cpsc.gov

International Association for Child Safety (IACS), *a non-profit organization, offers safety advice to parents, including referrals to child-safety professionals.*
P. O. Box 801
Summit, NJ 07902
Phone: 888-677-4227
www.iaf.com

Juvenile Products Manufacturers Association (JPMA), *a trade organization, represents makers of child-care products.*
17000 Commerce Pkwy., Ste. C
Mt. Laurel, NJ 08054
Phone: 856-638-0420
www.jpma.org

National Safety Council (NSC) *is a nonprofit public service organization.*
1121 Spring Lake Dr.
Itasca, IL 60143
Phone: 800-621-7619
www.nsc.org

Window Covering Safety Council *provides consumers with educational information including window-cord safety.*

355 Lexington Ave., Ste. 1700
New York, NY 10017
Phone: 800-506-4636
www.windowcoverings.org

MANUFACTURERS & DISTRIBUTORS

Bébé Sounds, *a division of Unisar, Inc., manufactures the Angel Care Monitor, Movement Sensor, Nursery Air Purifier, and other products.*
15 W. 36th St.
New York, NY 10018
Phone: 800-430-0222
www.bebesounds.com

Benjamin Moore & Co. *manufactures paint.*
51 Chestnut Ridge Rd.
Montvale, NJ 07645
www.benjaminmoore.com

Blonder Accents *manufactures wallcoverings and fabrics.*
3950 Prospect Ave.
Cleveland, OH 44115
Phone: 216-431-3560
www.blonderwall.com

Blue Mountain Wallcoverings, Inc., *manufactures wallcoverings under the brand names Imperial, Sunworthy, Katzenbach & Warren, and Sanitas.*
15 Akron Rd.
Toronto, ON M8W 1T3
Phone: 866-563-9872
www.imp-wall.com

CoCaLo, Inc., *manufactures juvenile bedding under the brand names CoCaLo, Oshkosh B' Gosh, Baby Martex, and Kimberly Grant.*
2920 Red Hill Ave.

Costa Mesa, CA 92626
Phone: 714-434-7200
www.cocalo.com

DuPont Stainmaster *manufactures stain-resistant carpeting.*
Phone: 800-438-7668
www.dupont.com/stainmaster

Enabling Devices *manufactures products and toys for children with special needs.*
385 Warburton Ave.
Hastings-on-Hudson, NY 10706
Phone: 800-832-8697
www.enablingdevices.com

Finn + Hattie, *a division of Maine Cottage, manufactures juvenile furniture.*
P.O. Box 539
Yarmouth, ME 04096
Phone: 207-846-9166
www.finnandhattie.com

Forever Mine *manufactures juvenile furnishings.*
14361 N. Dale Mabry
Tampa, FL 33618
Phone: 800-356-2742
www.forevermine.com

Graco *manufactures car seats, carriages, strollers, portable cribs, and accessories.*
150 Oaklands Blvd.
Exton, PA 19341
Phone: 800-345-4109
www.graco.com

Gund *manufactures plush toys.*
1 Runyons Ln.
Edison, NJ 08817
www.gund.com

RESOURCE GUIDE

Haier America, Inc., *manufactures dehumidifiers among other home appliances.*
1356 Broadway
New York, NY 10018
Phone: 877-377-3639
www.haieramerica.com

Hunter Douglas Window Fashions *manufactures window treatments, such as blinds and shades.*
2 Park Way
Upper Saddle River, NJ 07458
Phone: 800-789-0331
www.hunterdouglas.com

Ikea *manufactures furniture and accessories that are available in stores nationwide.*
www.ikea.com

Kids II *distributes safety products and toys.*
1015 Windward Ridge Pkwy.
Alpharetta, GA 30005
Phone: 770-751-0442
www.kidsii.com

Kolcraft *manufactures juvenile bedding.*
Phone: 800-453-7673
www.kolcraft.com

Lambs and Ivy *manufactures juvenile bedding, rugs, lamps, and accessories.*

5978 Bowcroft St.
Los Angeles, CA 90016
Phone: 800-345-2627
www.lambsandivy.com

Let's Learn Educational Toys, Inc., *manufactures educational toys for children.*
1 Slater Dr.
Elizabeth, NJ 07206
Phone: 908-629-9797
www.letslearntoys.com

Motif Designs *manufactures furniture, fabrics, and wallcoverings.*
20 Jones St.
New Rochelle, NY 10802
www.motif-designs.com

PatchKraft *manufactures coordinated bedding for cribs and twin- and full-size beds, using infant-safe fabrics.*
Phone: 800-866-2229
www.patchkraft.com

Plaid Industries *manufactures stencils, stamps, and craft paints.*
P.O. Box 7600
Norcross, GA 30091
Phone: 800-842-4197
www.plaidonline.com

Prince Lionheart, Inc., *manufactures Diaper Depot, Wipes Warmer, Slumber Bear, Crib Rail Teether, and more.*
2421 S. Westgate Rd.
Santa Maria, CA 93455
Phone: 805-922-2250
www.princelionheart.com

Seabrook Wallcoverings, Inc., *manufactures borders and wallcoverings.*
1325 Farmville Rd.
Memphis, TN 38122
Phone: 800-238-9152
www.seabrookwallpaper.com

Stencil Ease *manufactures laser-cut stencils and related tools and supplies.*
P.O. Box 1127
Old Saybrook, CT 06475
Phone: 800-334-1776
www.stencilease.com

TFH USA *manufactures toys and products for children with special needs.*
4537 Gibsonia Rd.
Gibsonia, PA 15044
Phone: 800-467-6222
www.tfhusa.com

The First Years *manufactures baby bathtubs, gates, monitors, and more.*
One Kiddie Dr.
Boston, MA 02322
Phone: 800-225-0382
www.thefirstyears.com

The Well Appointed House *sells and distributes juvenile furnishings nationwide.*
19 E. 65th St., Ste. 7B
New York, NY
Phone: 888-935-5277
www.wellappointedhouse.com

Thibaut *manufactures wallcovering, borders, and fabric.*
480 Frelinghuysen Ave.
Newark, NJ 07114
Phone: 800-223-0704
www.thibautdesign.com

Tots in Mind *manufactures crib tents and other baby- and toddler-related products.*
215 S. Broadway, Ste. 312
Salem, NH 03079
Phone:800-626-0339
www.totsinmind.com

Waverly Baby *manufactures bedding, wallcoverings, and window treatments for the nursery.*
79 Madison Ave.
New York, NY 10016
Phone: 800-423-5881
www.waverly.com

York Wallcoverings *manufactures borders and wallcoverings.*
700 Linden Ave.
York, PA 17404
Phone: 717-846-4456
www.yorkwall.com

GLOSSARY

Accessible Designs: Any design that accommodates persons with physical disabilities.

Acrylic Paint: A water-soluble paint with a plastic polymer (acrylic) binder.

Adaptable Designs: Any design that can be easily adjusted to accommodate a person with disabilities.

Analogous Scheme: See Harmonious Color Scheme.

Armoire: A large, often ornate, cupboard or wardrobe that is used for storage.

Asymmetry: As a decorating concept, the balance between different-sized objects, parts, or forms as the result of placement. An example of an asymmetrical arrangement is that of a window treatment consisting of a scarf valance that is draped over a curtain rod in such a way that the tail on one end is longer than the tail on the other end.

Audio and Video Monitor: A high-tech version of a baby monitor (below) that lets you see as well as hear your baby when you are not in the same room. Some versions combine a digital camera with a computer so that you can watch your baby through an Internet connection when you are away from home.

Baby Monitor: An electric or battery-powered device that consists of a transmitter and a receiver, which enables you to hear what is happening in the nursery when you are out of the room. Some monitors have walkie-talkie features, allowing you to talk to the baby from another location in and around the house.

Balance: As a decorating concept, the equilibrium among the objects or forms in a room that appears natural and comfortable to the eye. For example, two pictures of relatively equal size and weight balance each other and look pleasing as a pair on a wall. Balance can also apply to color or other aspects of the elements in a room.

Bassinet: A newborn baby's bed that is shaped like a basket with a hood at one end. A bassinet is light-weight and traditionally made of wicker, although it can also be made of plastic. A bassinet has a stand with wheels or castors that lock for safety.

Built-in: Any element, such as a bookcase or cabinetry, that is built into a wall or an existing frame.

Bumpers: Padded cushions that are attached to the side rails of a crib.

Case Goods: Furniture used for storage, including cabinets, dressers, and desks.

Chaise Longue: A chair with back support and a seat long enough for outstretched legs.

Changing Table: A stand-alone padded table that is used for changing the baby. Some changing tables are dressers with an attached or portable raised deck that is equipped with a pad. The deck can be removed when a changing table is no longer needed.

Clearance: The amount of space between two fixtures, the centerlines of two fixtures, or a fixture and an obstacle, such as a wall. Clearances may be mandated by codes.

Code: A locally or nationally enforced mandate regarding structural design, materials, plumbing, or electrical systems that state what you can or cannot do when you build or remodel. Codes are intended to protect standards of health, safety, and land use.

Color Scheme: A group of colors used together to create visual harmony in a space.

Color Wheel: A pie-shaped diagram showing the range and relationships of pigment and dye colors. Three equidistant wedge-shaped slices are the primary colors; in between are the secondary and tertiary colors into which the primaries combine. Though represented as discrete slices, the hues form a continuum.

Complementary Colors: Hues directly opposite each other on the color wheel. As the strongest con-

trasts, complementary colors tend to intensify each other. A color can be grayed by mixing it with its complement.

Contemporary: Any modern design (after 1920) that does not contain or refer to traditional elements of the past.

Convertible Crib: A crib that converts to a junior bed or a twin- or full-size bed.

Contrast: The art of assembling colors with different values and intensities and in different proportions to create a dynamic scheme.

Cradle: An infant's bed that is made of wood and has rockers.

Crib Railings: The usually slatted enclosures on both sides of a crib that can be adjusted to a high or low position. Slats should be spaced no more than $2^3/_8$ inches apart to prevent accidents.

Daybed: A bed made up to appear as a sofa. It usually has a frame that consists of a headboard, a footboard, and a sideboard along the back.

Dehumidifier: A device that reduces the amount of moisture in the air without cooling it.

Floor Plan: A layout of a room that has been drawn to scale.

Focal Point: The dominant element in a room or design, usually the first to catch your eye.

Genuine Wood Furniture: A label on a piece of furniture indicating that all of the exposed parts are made of a veneer (of a specified wood) over hardwood plywood.

Hardware: Wood, plastic, or metal-plated trim found on the exterior of furniture, such as knobs, handles, locks, hinges, and decorative trim.

Harmony: As a decorating concept, harmony is the continuity between the different elements of a room. For example, sleek unfettered designs are harmonious with contemporary architecture.

Harmonious Color Scheme: Also called analogous, a combination focused on neighboring hues on the color wheel. The shared underlying color generally gives such schemes a coherent flow.

Hue: Specific points on the pure, clear range of the color wheel. Also, another term for color.

Incandescent Lamp: A bulb that contains a conductive filament through which current flows. The current reacts with an inert gas inside the bulb, which makes the filament glow.

Indirect Lighting: A subdued type of lighting that is not head-on, but reflected against another surface, such as a ceiling.

Innerspring Mattress: A coil mattress. The higher the coil count, the more support it provides. The

minimum coil count for a crib mattress is 150. Twin-size mattresses should have at least 200 coils.

Junior Bed: A transitional bed for a toddler. A junior bed, also known as a "youth bed," uses a crib-size mattress. Some cribs convert to a junior bed.

Laminate: One or more thin layers of durable plastic that is bonded to a fabric or a material. It may used on furniture, countertops, and floors.

Latex Paint: A water-soluble, quick-drying paint that contains either acrylic or vinyl resins or a combination of the two. High-quality latex paints contain 100-percent acrylic resin.

Man-made Materials: A furniture label that refers to plastic-laminate panels that are printed to look like wood. The furniture may also include plastic that has been molded to look like wood carving or trim.

Mobile: A mechanical wheel with suspended shapes that hangs above the crib or over the changing table. A wind-up mechanism or battery-operated device sets the mobile in motion and activates optional sound features.

Modular Furniture: Units of a standard size, such as chests, dressers, and hutches, that are not built-in and can be used separately or fitted together in a number of arrangements.

Molding: An architectural band that can either trim a line where materials join or create a linear decoration at the top of a cabinet or on the wall. It is typically made of wood, but metal, plaster, or polymer (plastic) is also used.

Natural Fibers: Any fibers or fabrics that are not man-made. These include cotton, linen, wool, and silk.

Orientation: The placement of any object or space, such as a window, door, or room, and its relationship to the points on a compass.

Overall: A term for a pattern on fabric or wallcovering that is even and overall or random. An overall pattern is most commonly used on curtains.

Palette: See Color Scheme.

Panel: A flat, rectangular piece of material that forms part of a wall, door, or cabinet. Typically made of wood, it is usually framed by a border and either raised or recessed.

Parquet: Inlaid woodwork arranged to form a geometric pattern on a floor. It consists of small blocks of hardwood, which are often stained in contrasting colors.

Pattern Matching: To align a repeating pattern when joining together two pieces of fabric or wallpaper.

Pocket Door: A door that slides into the wall when it is open.

Polyurethane: A tough, hard-wearing coating made of synthetic resins. It serves as a good top coat or finish and can be applied over most types of painted- or stained-wood surfaces, such as furniture or floors. Non-yellowing polyester produces a clear finish.

Primary Color: Red, blue, or yellow, which can't be produced in pigments by mixing other colors. Primaries plus black and white, in turn, combine to make all the other hues.

Primer: A coating that prepares surfaces for painting by making them more uniform in texture and giving them "tooth."

Proportion: The relationship of parts or objects to one another based on size. For example, the size of a baby's shoes is in proportion to the size of her feet.

Readymade: A term used to describe something that has been mass-produced in standard sizes, such as curtains or slipcovers.

Rhythm: A decorating concept that refers to any form of repetition that coordinates visual elements. For example, repeated patterns, colors, or themes.

Sample: A small piece or cutting from a roll of wallcovering or a bolt of fabric that is used to test at home or as a reference for coordinating colors and prints.

Sample Board: A small, typically foam-cored board that is used to hold and try out swatches, samples, and color chips. The various samples should be displayed on the board in proportion to how they would appear in the room for an accurate evaluation of the projected overall design.

Safety Gate: A barrier that can be mounted to walls or installed in door and window frames to keep a baby from wandering or from injury.

Scale: The size of something as it relates to the size of everything else. For example, babies are small, adults are large.

Sealer: A coating that is applied to porous surfaces before painting in order to form a durable, non-absorbent barrier between the surface and the paint. A sealer facilitates a smooth and even finish.

Secondary Color: A mix of two primaries. The secondary colors are orange, green, and purple.

Sensor Pad: A feature of some baby monitors, a sensor pad is a thin, almost flat transmitter that fits under the crib mattress. It detects the slightest movements of a baby, sounds an alarm, and signals the receiver if the infant is absolutely motionless for more than 20 seconds.

Shade: A color to which black or gray has been added to make it darker.

Sheen: The quality of paint that reflects light when it is dry. It can range from matted (completely non-reflective) to high gloss (very shiny).

Stencil: A cut-out pattern.

Solid Wood: A furniture label indicating that the exposed surfaces are made of wood without any veneer or plywood.

Sudden Infant Death Syndrome (SIDS): The sudden death of a baby under 1 year old.

Swatch: A cutting or sample of a piece of fabric.

Symmetry: The exact arrangement of objects, parts, or forms on both sides of an imagined or real center line. An example of a symmetrical arrangement is that of a window treatment consisting of a scarf valance that is draped over a curtain rod in such a way that the tails on either side are the same length.

Synthetic Fibers: Man-made alternatives to natural fibers. Examples include polyester, nylon, rayon, and acetate.

Stenciling: Creating an image or a motif, often in a repeated pattern, by painting a cut-out pattern.

Ticking: A strong, closely woven cotton that usually has stripes.

Tint: A color to which white or light gray has been added to make it lighter.

Tone: The degree of lightness or darkness of a color. A color to which gray has been added to change its value.

Trompe L'oeil: Literally meaning "fool the eye;" a painted mural in which realistic images and the illusion three-dimensional space are created. Also, a painted surface that convincingly mimics reality.

Youth Bed: See Junior Bed.

Value: In relation to a scale of grays ranging from black to white, the lightness (tints) or darkness (shades) of a color.

Veneer: High-quality wood that is cut into very thin sheets for use as a surface material—on a piece of furniture, for example.

Wainscoting: Traditionally, paneling or woodwork that covers the lower third of the wall.

Wash: A thinned-out latex or acrylic paint.

Welt: A cord, often covered with fabric, that is used to trim cushions or slipcovers.

Wood: A furniture label that indicates that none of the parts of the furniture are made of plastic, metal, or anything other than wood.

INDEX

PHOTO CREDITS

All Photography: Mark Samu, unless otherwise noted.

pages 1, 2, 6, & 8: courtesy of York Wallcoverings **page 9:** courtesy of The First Years **pages 10 & 11:** courtesy of York Wallcoverings **page 12:** designer: Picture Perfect Design **page 13:** *bottom* courtesy of PatchKraft **page 19:** *top* designer: Picture Perfect Design; *bottom* courtesy of Seabrook Wallcoverings **page 24:** *bottom left* & *bottom right* courtesy of PatchKraft **page 25:** courtesy of PatchKraft **pages 26 & 27:** *top left* & *center* courtesy of Gund; *top right* courtesy of Waverly; *bottom left* courtesy of Lambs & Ivy **page 28:** courtesy of Seabrook Wallcoverings **page 29:** *top left* & *top right* by Lyn Peterson for Motif Designs; *bottom* courtesy of PatchKraft **pages 30 & 31:** *top left* designer: Ken Kelly; *top right* & *bottom right* by Lyn Peterson for Motif Designs; *center* courtesy of Gund; *bottom left* by Lyn Peterson for Motif Designs **page 32:** courtesy of Benjamin Moore & Co. **page 33:** *all* courtesy of York Wallcoverings **page 35:** courtesy of Benjamin Moore & Co. **pages 36 & 37:** courtesy of Seabrook Wallcoverings **page 38:** courtesy of York Wallcoverings **page 39:** courtesy of CoCaLo/Osh Gosh B' Gosh **pages 41 & 42:** courtesy of York Wallcoverings **page 43:** *top center* courtesy of CoCaLo/Osh Gosh B' Gosh; *bottom* courtesy of Seabrook Wallcoverings **page 44:** *top right* courtesy of Seabrook **page 45:** courtesy of CoCaLo/Baby Martex **page 46:** courtesy of Blue Mountain Wallcoverings **page 47:** *center* designer: Picture Perfect Design; *bottom* courtesy of York Wallcoverings **page 48:** *top left* courtesy of Gund **page 49:** courtesy of York Wallcoverings **page 51:** designer: Ken Kelly **page 52:** courtesy of York Wallcoverings **page 53:** *top* designer: Mari Gardner Design **page 56:** courtesy of Gund **page 57:** *top* courtesy of Hunter Douglas **page 59:** courtesy of PatchKraft **page 60:** courtesy of Lambs & Ivy **page 61:** *top left* & *bottom left* by Lyn Peterson for Motif Designs **page 62:** *bottom left* by Lyn Peterson for Motif Designs **page 63:** by Lyn Peterson for Motif Designs **page 66:** *top* by Lyn Peterson for Motif Designs **page 78:** *bottom right* courtesy of Rubbermaid **page 83:** *left column (top to bottom)* courtesy of Rubbermaid **page 84:** courtesy of York Wallcoverings **page 85:** *top* courtesy of York Wallcoverings; *center* courtesy of Kids II **page 86:** courtesy of York Wallcoverings **page 87:** *bottom* courtesy of The Well Appointed House **page 88:** *top* courtesy of York Wallcoverings **pages 95 & 96:** courtesy of York Wallcoverings **page 98:** *top right* & *center right* courtesy of Waverly **page 99:** courtesy of York Wallcoverings **page 100:** courtesy of Seabrook Wallcoverings **page 101:** *top* by Lyn Peterson for Motif Designs **page 102 & 103:** *bottom center* & *top right* by Lyn Peterson for Motif Designs; **page 104:** courtesy of York Wallcoverings **page 105:** *top* designer: Mari Gardner; *bottom* architect: Jim Deluca, AIA **page 106:** *top* courtesy of Thibaut **page 107:** courtesy of Stencil Ease **page 108:** *bottom* designer: Picture Perfect Design **pages 109 & 111:** courtesy of York Wallcoverings **page 116:** *top* courtesy of Hunter Douglas; *bottom* designer: East End Interiors **page 117:** *top* designer: Mari Gardner Design; *bottom* courtesy of York Wallcoverings **page 118:** *top* designer: Pat Hildenbrand Design **page 119:** courtesy of Blue Mountain Wallcoverings **pages 120 & 121:** *center* courtesy of York Wallcoverings **page 122:** courtesy of Thibaut **page 124:** courtesy of Seabrook Wallcoverings **page 125:** *top* & *bottom right* courtesy of York Wallcoverings **page 126:** *top left* & *top right* by Lyn Peterson for Motif Designs; *bottom right* & *bottom left* courtesy of Seabrook Wallcoverings **page 127:** courtesy of York Wallcoverings **page 128:** architect: Jim Deluca, AIA **page 129:** *top* courtesy of Forever Mine; *center* courtesy of Lambs & Ivy; *bottom* designer: Anne Tarasoff **page 130:** designer: Painted Pieces **page 131:** courtesy of Finn & Hattie **page 132:** architect: Ellen Roche, AIA, room designer: Lucianna Samu **page 133:** *right* designer: Painted Pieces **page 134:** courtesy of Finn + Hattie **page 135:** *top* designer: Anne Tarasoff; *bottom* designer: Jim Deluca, AIA **pages 138 & 139:** courtesy of The Well Appointed House **page 141:** courtesy of Ikea **page 142:** courtesy of Finn + Hattie **page 143:** *bottom* by Lyn Peterson for Motif Designs **page 144:** *top left* courtesy of Kids II; *bottom left* courtesy of Lambs & Ivy **page 145:** *top right* courtesy of Finn + Hattie; *bottom right* courtesy of Lambs & Ivy; *bottom left* courtesy of York Wallcoverings **page 147:** *all* Lambs & Ivy **page 148:** courtesy of Bébé Sounds **page 149:** *bottom* courtesy of The First Years **page 150:** courtesy of PatchKraft **page 151:** courtesy of Prince Lionheart **page 152:** *top right* courtesy of The Well Appointed House; *bottom right* The First Years; *bottom left* Lambs & Ivy **page 153:** courtesy of Lambs & Ivy **pages 154 & 155:** *top center* & *bottom right* courtesy of Prince Lionheart **pages 156 & 157:** *top left* courtesy of Gund; *top right* courtesy of Kids II; *center right* courtesy of The Well Appointed House; *bottom right* courtesy of Kids II; *bottom center* courtesy of Graco **page 158:** *top left* & *bottom right* courtesy of The Well Appointed House; *bottom left* courtesy of Kids II **page 159:** courtesy of Seabrook Wallcoverings **page 161:** *bottom left* courtesy of Bébé Sounds **page 162:** courtesy of Seabrook **page 163:** *all* courtesy of Lambs & Ivy **page 164:** courtesy of The Well Appointed House **page 165:** *top* courtesy of Prince Lionheart; *bottom* courtesy of PatchKraft **page 166:** courtesy of York Wallcoverings **page 167:** courtesy of Tots In Mind **pages 168 & 169:** courtesy of Finn + Hattie **page 171:** courtesy of Seabrook Wallcoverings **page 172:** courtesy of CoCaLo/Kimberly Grant **page 173:** *top left* courtesy of Kids II; *top right* courtesy of The First Years; *bottom right* courtesy of Tots In Mind; *bottom left* courtesy of Prince Lionheart; *center left* courtesy of Forever Mine **page 174:** courtesy of Seabrook Wallcoverings **page 175:** *top* & *center* courtesy of The First Years; *bottom* courtesy of courtesy of Enabling Devices **page 176:** *right* Enabling Devices **page 177:** courtesy of Blue Mountain Wallcoverings **page 178:** courtesy of Forever Mine **page 179:** courtesy of Bébé Sounds **pages 180 & 181:** *left* courtesy of Forever Mine **page 182:** *top* courtesy of Haier America, Inc.; *bottom* courtesy of The First Years **page 183:** courtesy of Seabrook Wallcoverings **pages 184 & 185:** *top left* courtesy of Forever Mine; *top right* courtesy of Ikea; *bottom row* courtesy of Enabling Devices

Have a home decorating, improvement, or gardening project? Look for these and other fine **Creative Homeowner books** wherever books are sold.

Ideas for furnishing and decorating space for children. Over 200 color photos. 176 pp., 9"×10"
BOOK #: 279473

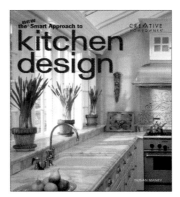

How to work with space, color, pattern, and texture. Over 440 photos. 288 pp.; 9"×10"
BOOK #: 279672

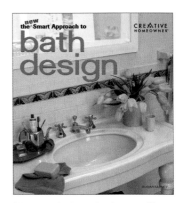

How to create a kitchen like a pro. Over 260 color photographs. 208 pp.; 9"×10"
Book #: 279946

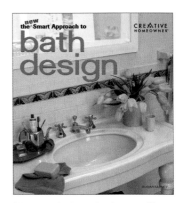

How to design a bathroom like the experts. Over 260 color photos. 208 pp.; 9"×10"
BOOK #: 279234

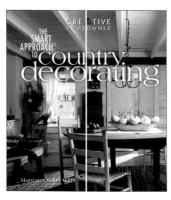

Explores new and traditional country decorating. More than 200 color photos.176 pp.; 9"×10"
BOOK #: 279685

Learn how to use color to transform a room. More than 200 color photos. 176 pp.; 9"×10"
BOOK #: 287264

Plan and select the perfect window treatment. 250 color photos. 208 pp., 9"×10"
BOOK #: 279438

Interior designer Lyn Peterson's easy-to-live-with decorating ideas. Over 300 photos. 304 pp., 9"×10"
BOOK #: 279382

A guide to paint techniques and faux finishes. More than 300 color photos. 240 pp.; 8½"×10⅞" w/flaps
BOOK #: 279020

Provides design advice for gaining functional basement space. Over 200 photos. 144 pp.; 8½"×10⅞"
BOOK #: 279430

How to use moldings and trim. Over 450 full-color photos and illustrations. 208 pp.; 8½"×10⅞"
Book #: 277495

How to tile floors, walls, and more. More than 450 color photos and illustrations. 160 pp.; 8½"×10⅞"
BOOK #: 277524

For more information, and to order direct, call 800-631-7795; in New Jersey 201-934-7100.
www.creativehomeowner.com